THE
ADIRONDACK
CABIN

The Adirondack Cabin

Robbin Obomsawin

Photographs by Nancie Battaglia

Gibbs Smith, Publisher
Salt Lake City

First Edition
08 07 06 05 04   5 4 3 2 1

Stock plans and reproducible masters of plans can be purchased with a license
through the design professional who created them. Please respect the design copy-
rights, as the designers have taken years to develop the designs and their stock plans
that specialize in the unusual form of construction.

The information in this book is intended to motivate and enrich the reader's think-
ing. It is not a guide for building. The drawings in the book are conceptual plans
and should not to be construed as construction drawings, nor may the descriptions
contained within be presented to or relied upon by an engineer, architect, designer
or construction professional.

The methods, designs and details shown in this book are not intended to be appropri-
ate in all situations and should be assessed and verified by a qualified professional,
ensuring their safety, durability and appropriateness for the individual situation and
compliance with applicable codes and regional building regulations as well as
statewide regulations. The author and publisher bear no responsibility for any out-
come resulting from practical application of any idea in this book.

Published by
Gibbs Smith, Publisher
P.O. Box 667
Layton, Utah 84041
Orders: 1.800.748.5439
www.gibbs-smith.com

Designed by Rudy Ramos
Printed and bound in Hong Kong

Library of Congress Cataloging-in-Publication Data
Obomsawin, Robbin, 1960-
  The adirondack cabin / Robbin Obomsawin ; photographs by Nancie Battaglia.—
1st ed.
     p. cm.
  ISBN 1-58685-741-X
  1 Camps—New York (State)—Adirondack Mountains Region. 2. Log cabins—New
York (State)—Adirondack Mountains Region. 3 Vernacular architecture—New York
(State)—Adirondack Mountains Region. 4 Decoration and ornament, Rustic—New
York (State)—Adirondack Mountains Region. I Battaglia, Nancie. II. Title.
NA7575.O36 2005
728'.09747'5—dc22
                                                        2004021515

Contents

Acknowledgments

I want to thank Nancie Battaglia for sharing her years of photography of the Adirondack landscape, activities, culture and architecture. Her patience and dedication of photography capture the Adirondacks at present and for future generations, gifting photographs that freeze a moment in time for a glimpse of our history in the making. I thank you for taking the time to work with me, as it is your photos that bring my words to life. I had such fun yet a very hard time selecting the perfect photographs

Adirondack chairs have a casual design with a slanted back and wide arms that comfortably hold a tall glass of lemonade or a cup of cocoa. Here, the glow of the red chair is in brilliant contrast to the wild flowers in the meadow.

to represent the Adirondacks. There were so many more great photos of the Adirondack land-scape that I wanted to share with the world but just did not have enough room within one book.

To Scott, Alice, Bob, and Lynn Patchett and family at the Trout House Village Resort, who have put us up on many occasions in one of their Adirondack rental camps so that we could spend some time photographing and writing about the Adirondack love affair with nature, we would have never had the opportunity to create this book without the generosity of accom-modations at the Patchett family resort. Their love and dedication to bring quality camps and cabins to those who have the need to escape the mad rush of life is commendable, providing retreats that give the chance to absorb

A fiddler perches on an Adirondack chair at the edge of serene Lake Placid. The clouds open to reveal Whiteface Mountain.

8   The Adirondack Cabin

the natural beauty of the Adirondacks. For this, we are greatly thankful and appreciative.

To my clients who have been so good to our log-building crews and design staff. It is your enthusiasm and love of architecture that has made our projects shine. We appreciate your patience and respect of our work to create the level of design and detail we have been able to achieve. We are also grateful for your willingness to share these design details with the world, which will hopefully inspire others. A special thanks to all the families who live year-round in the Adirondacks and help in some way as caretakers of such a great resource. You have my thanks and appreciation in caring for such a pristine slice of nature—it is a special honor.

A cabin nestled on Lake Placid has a stunning view of the mountains.

Introduction

Nothing can capture our hearts and imaginations quite the same as the pure simplicity of an Adirondack camp. It is without a doubt the most refined rustic form of architecture. The use of natural materials with their myriad imperfections creates the ironic effect of perfection itself. Many designers and homeowners have fallen in love with and borrowed the Adirondack style of architecture and interior design to use in their homes the world over because its rustic décor is casual, yet romantic.

Browsing through Adirondack furnishings is a real treat at the Ray Brook Frog. Lettering on the birch bark signs are formed out of twigs, and birch bark is also used for a rustic lampshade. Most of the sticking or sewing is done with ash strips, which are made by pounding a black ash raw log with a mallet. This separates the straight grain of the log fiber and creates thin strips of pliable wood. Fragrant sweet grass is often used at the bases and tops of the picture frames and lamps as decorative "cording" or piping.

*An evening campfire takes the chill off the
cool night while roasting marshmallows and
telling Adirondack ghost stories and lore.*

Even from a distance, the Adirondack camp radiates romance as it wraps itself in spectacular terrain. It is a love affair with nature that has caused this form of architecture and design to be so popular in many areas.

It is our ideal human experience to integrate nature into every possible aspect of daily living, where man and nature can coexist in harmony with one another. The Adirondack architectural style is one in which the structure blends with nature's own structural décor. This age-old design has stood the test of time and continues to remain a classic. This symbiotic arrangement allows us the chance to live in harmony with nature as well as give back to the land. It is our individual spirits that bring life into a home and our passion and dedication that creates what each of us considers the "perfect" home.

During the early twentieth century, *Adirondack great camps* were established by wealthy rail and oil barons such as the Vanderbilts and the Rockefellers, who wanted to get away and enjoy nature to its fullest. These camp structures incorporated natural materials into

The initials for Breezy Point are crafted out of twigs and saplings to crown the camp's entry. Each twig is carefully scribed and back cut to each other to give a fitted appearance, as if they had grown that way.

every aspect of the constructions in an effort to create a complete natural effect. These camps were very large with every amenity. The old great camps were often self-contained with their own water faculties, electrical generating plants and a full staff of caretakers, gardeners and servants. The great camps were often so elaborate, with dancing halls, bowling alleys, servant quarters, multiple guest-houses and outdoor pavilions. Although not all of us want or need a large, ornate camp to enjoy nature, we can create our own modern-day great camp, where the simplicity of nature itself echoes throughout our modest dwellings. The great camps of today are designed to not compete with nature but to work with it by blending in with the natural land-scapes and disturbing the environ-ment as little as possible. The Adirondack tradition is to build

The quiet on the lake allows visitors a chance for solitude and reflection.

and design camps that respect, protect and preserve Mother Nature. What a wonderful gift and privilege to be her caretaker, even if for just a short period of time.

The Adirondack Mountains' rustic beauty is very hard to capture in words, photographs or drawings. The best way to pick up the real essence of this unique environment is to actually live with its ruggedness at its best and at its worst. The brutal winters with heavy snow, ice and winds are balanced with nature's crystal ice castles and soft blankets of snow. The springs plagued with black flies and mosquitoes that seem as large as birds are offset by summer's most perfect weather, the tranquil call of the loon, and the teasing trill of crickets and frogs. Many generations of loggers, miners, furriers, artisans and craftsmen have lived year-round in the Adirondacks, but today most of its population is comprised of summer vacationers and part-time residents who own or rent a small part of the

Adirondack landscape. The Adirondack rock formations, mountains and lakes take one's breath away and will inspire even the sourest of souls.

The Adirondack Cabin focuses on the new hybrid forms of log-element architecture along with traditionally crafted, more whimsical and romantic camps for a new generation of *woodsmen* who wish to capture these Adirondack forms of architecture. These builders are often skilled craftsmen in their own right, with years of experience constructing handcrafted structures using all forms of traditional joinery methods. This book provides a resource for builders, design professionals, and others who are equally fascinated by a study or glimpse of the Adirondack region's natural features and design details that create these smaller but magical great camps of today. These camps are comprised of a mix of log cabins and log-element structures of 1,500 square feet and less. All of these structures can be built off the land and are in harmony with nature and in respect of the surroundings.

This photographic tour of the Adirondacks is not just about homes but also about the landscape that creates the Adirondacks. I feel that the kaleidoscope of landscape, craftsmen, homeowners, and Adirondack activities and sports are just as important to the creation of a home's design, as these all influence the Adirondack style.

I am pleased to feature the photographs of Nancie Battaglia, who is well known and highly respected in the area. She has spent many years living in and capturing the essence of the Adirondacks, which she shares through her camera's eye. This is just a small glimpse of the microscopic part of this great country's diversity, landscape and personalities. We also included within the photography some wonderful Adirondack chairs that have distinctive shapes, forms, colors and signature styles, because what would an Adirondack camp be without Adirondack chairs?

My design staff and I have put our hearts and souls into the great camps featured in this book. We have combined our years of experience, practical building knowledge and passion for the traditional forms of architecture to capture camp designs and photographs that effectively demonstrate how one can put nature back into its architecture. These are camp designs that interact with nature, and may be a good starting point for your great camp odyssey or may serve as encouragement for your own ideas. I wish you inspiration in this book's journey through nature's own Adirondacks.

Opposite: Wild iris by Alford Pond views across to Seymour Mountain.

Details of Adirondack Great Camps

The new hybrids of log architecture are not so new to the Adirondacks. Log elements and accents have been incorporated into Adirondack camps since the very origin of camps. The Iroquois construction process in their longhouse architecture used what was needed from the land and largely influenced the earliest of nonindigenous camps. The Adirondack style was also influenced by ornate Victorian style and stripped-down simplicity of the Arts and Crafts movement popular at the turn of

A small camp is all that is needed for large amounts of fun. The camp is wrapped in fall color that glows in the background. The roof has a wonderful patina of natural rust.

the century. This most unusual fusion of eclectic characteristics evolved into the Adirondack style, made famous through the Adirondack great camps being built in the same time period.

Great camps in the Adirondacks from the 1870s to the 1930s were built by the wealthy on only a seasonal basis. The Adirondack Mountains were left unexplored until not so long ago. The region became an interest to those in New York City, as it was only two hundred miles to the north, and the natural beauty and abundant hunting and fishing of the Adirondacks were attractive features.

Those wealthy enough constructed elaborate wilderness camps to escape the overcrowded cities, building complex structures in the middle of the hostile Adirondack

Every artist has a distinctive style in creating the perfect Adirondack chair. The snow-dusted chairs give a hint of the long Adirondack winter ahead.

environment. Each camp became a reflection of the owners' wealth and interests. It became a quest to tame the surrounding environment. These forms of rustic Adirondack architecture were built for roughing it, yet the best crystal and silver were required.

* * *

Many journalists romanticized the log cabin and log-element forms of Adirondack architecture of the turn of the century. The romantic, rustic style became an influence throughout many mountainous regions that inspired many national forest building designs, such as Yellowstone Lodge in the Rocky

Small details combine to give an overall Adirondack feel. Notice the coffee table's unique edging that mimics the vertical siding found on many cabins. The chair backs are tied in traditional snowshoe patterns.

Mountains. The rustic, sometimes whimsical Adirondack style was also used in many privately owned structures in the Great Lakes region, Appalachian Mountains, New England Mountains and the western slopes of the Rockies.

The Adirondack form of architecture was sculpted and interpreted out of many cultures, including the local indigenous Indian cultures of the Iroquois and the neighboring Canadian Abenaki of the north. Their native craftsmanship made use of hemlock, birch twig and sapling materials; these were common materials used in traditional longhouse construction. The rough terrain and remote locations required ingenuity in using these raw materials. These techniques were modified to fit the conventional framed structures cut from local mills.

This area's architecture was also influenced by wood joinery methods

Opposite: Vertical siding appears simple, yet it is a labor-intensive application compared to other methods of siding. Nothing is quite as rustic and woodsy in appearance as this unique style.

Above: Pendleton blankets add color to the natural materials used to form the bed's headboard and twig nightstand.

from imported carpenters from many other countries working in the Adirondack fur, mining and lumber trades. Other influences were made by owners' extensive travels and publications inspired by European, Scandinavian, German, Russian and Japanese carpentry methods.

Most of the region's camps and cabins were not large great camps but only small cabins, trapper's shacks and lean-tos. Often the camps and cabins were only one to one-and-a-half stories with a fireplace at one end for cooking and heating. Minimal windows were installed in order to retain the cabin's heat. To add additional protection during the long periods of rain and snow, porches and large roof overhangs were used to protect the logs, lumber and natural materials from the harsh elements of the Adirondack region. The limitations and accessibility of materials compared to their great camp cousins often influenced this conservative camp architecture. When constructed well, these pint-size camps and cabins were just as beautiful and grand in their own way.

The circular windows and diamond-pane grilles are set into the vertical siding. The railings are built in a free-form style of twig art construction.

Opposite: A set of red Westport Adirondack chairs at The Point, an exclusive retreat and lodge.

Traditional Joinery Styles

Many older and newer handcrafted log structures can tell their origins of influence based on joinery techniques or a signature style that an individual builder developed or passed down through generations of builders. Many of these traditional joinery styles have either not changed or changed very little over the years. Today's handcrafted log-building methods still primarily use the same hand-held tools and techniques that make the process a labor-intensive endeavor. There have been adaptations and new technologies that different builders share and techniques that have somewhat unified the handcrafted building techniques throughout the world.

Although the Adirondack great camps of yesterday are great legends of extraordinary architecture, today's Adirondack great camps are becoming much more conservative by choice. Mindfully considerate for our overbearance on the landscape, these smaller, downsized great camps are today's small treasures in tomorrow's history. It becomes a difficult balance to maintain this living museum of untamed wilderness. This untouched slice of nature can be a sobering reminder of what once existed.

The great camps of today are small jewels, less formal or elaborate than their early ancestors. They are sculptures created by builders who enjoy the art of construction and not the mass production of today's typical housing market.

The distinctive style of Adirondack architecture has several common features. These are mostly natural materials found within the region known for its abundance of raw logs, machined lumber, twigs, log saplings, iron mines and stone cropping. We will go through various design details and examine how they affect a home's form and function. These added structural elements lend personality, sizzle and "beef" to any plain-Jane structure. The essence of an Adirondack structure lies in the natural components that are incorporated. Accents of large logs and branches can allow for dramatic spaces and unique features for those craving a bit of log therapy or "twig-onometry."

A view of Lake Placid from the top of Whiteface Mountain.

27

The steam rolls off the water while an angler fly fishes on the Au Sable River.

The areas of a camp that can incorporate log elements or accents are railings, stairs, trusses, and floor or ceiling joists. A thorough explanation that details these log-element construction styles and methods and how they are used are featured in my book *The Not So Log Cabin*, which includes valuable drawings, photos and floor plans of many different styles of log-element architecture, from Adirondack whimsy to Southwest tradition and cowboy chic.

Adirondack Weather

The Adirondacks have brief summers with extended spring and summer rains driven by lateral winds that have carved the rugged terrain. It is hard to convince a short-time visitor of the unpredictability of the Adirondack weather. Locals know it is not uncommon to start a fire on August mornings and in the evenings to take the chill out of the air. Rains can last for weeks while blizzards can drop out of perfectly sunny skies.

Many architectural features in the Adirondacks reflect these extreme weather conditions. Whether it is seen in the exterior or interior details, Adirondack architecture must always consider the area's climate.

Distinctive Architectural Exteriors

Many Adirondack structures are conventionally built stick-frame structures sometimes emphasized with only log or timber accents. The siding choices are limitless—stone, stucco, and wood sidings of many forms such as shingles, clapboard, board and batten, shiplap, wanes board, and tongue and groove are mixed and matched. But within an Adirondack structure it is the use of log elements, twig accents and natural materials that are sculpted into the camp's exterior that creates this distinctive style.

The vertical log siding on the second story loft
alternates between a large log and a small log.
This unique pattern mimics the forest trees.

A wanes board–sided camp with a diamond birch board inlay pattern.

Opposite: At the Adirondack Museum in Blue Mountain Lake, Sunset Cottage is designed with twig art siding sculpted in patterns and sunburst designs.

- *Adirondack siding* is unique to Adirondack architecture, where the tree is milled on only three sides, leaving the one natural-shaped edge exposed. This allows the various limb protrusions and contours to be featured, creating a natural wave and a more free-formed edge. (See detailed drawing on page 35.)

- *Vertical log siding* is created with one- or two-year-old tree saplings. The bark may or may not be left intact, depending on the time of year and the species of wood used. Unlike milled siding, where the boards are cut from large logs with flat surfaces, vertical log siding is created from small-diameter trees left in their natural round form on the exposed surface. (See detailed drawing on pages 22, 25, 31, 33 and 36.)

Each tree creates an individual texture and pattern on its bark. Birch bark is typically white and yellow, with variations created by flecks of other colors created by molds and fungi that range from red and yellow to orange and greens hues.

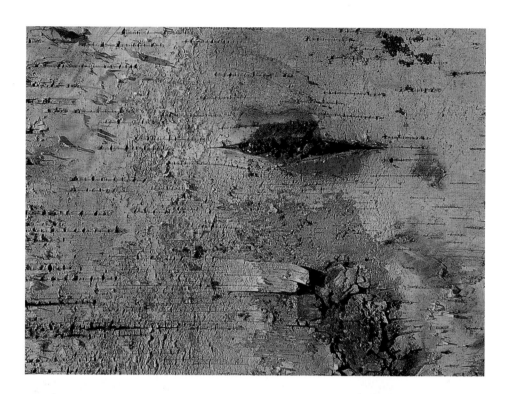

EXAMPLE OF WAIN BOARD SIDING
WITH STONE BASE

• *Elm bark* is skinned from a large-diameter elm tree in one massive sheet for use as sheathing. Even after years of storage, it can still be made pliable by soaking the bark to reform it to many configurations.

• *Birch bark* may also be used as sheathing and is usually peeled, or the tree is debarked in spring and summer, when the bark has plenty of sap under its surface for easy removal (winter bark is much more difficult to peel). The flaky white outer bark gives the cabin a fresh, bright, fairy tale look and creates quite a depth of texture.

• *Large diameter timbers* carved and sculpted by specialized craftsmen are used to create traditional handcrafted log cabins.

Throughout American history, log cabins have graced our landscape. When built well these handcrafted log cabins classics stand as a testament to the constitution and warmth of wood and its timeless beauty.

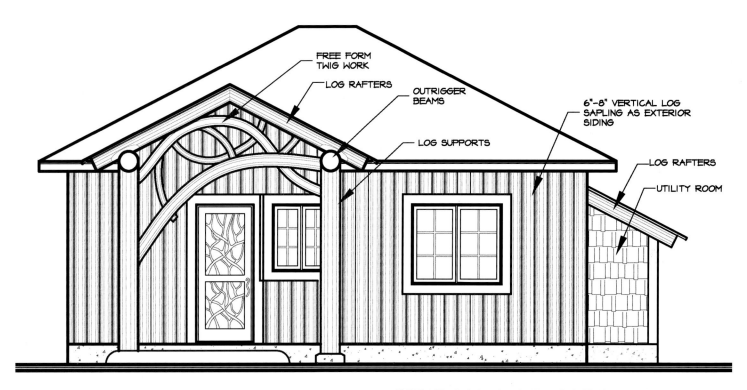

FREE FORM
TWIG WORK

LOG RAFTERS

OUTRIGGER
BEAMS

6"-8" VERTICAL LOG
SAPLING AS EXTERIOR
SIDING

LOG SUPPORTS

LOG RAFTERS

UTILITY ROOM

VERTICAL LOG CABIN WALLS
WITH SHINGLE SIDED UTILITY ROOM

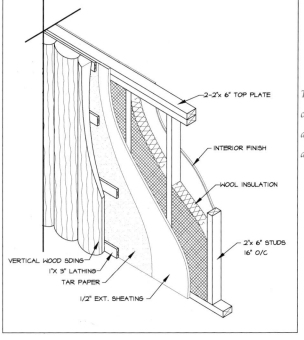

2-2"x 6" TOP PLATE

INTERIOR FINISH

WOOL INSULATION

2"x 6" STUDS
16" O/C

VERTICAL WOOD SDING
I"X 3" LATHING
TAR PAPER
1/2" EXT. SHEATING

To create the artfully rustic look of vertical log siding, builders can choose from many methods. Depending on the skill level and experience of the craftsperson, a variety of looks can be achieved. Here is one example of siding.

Bark

Canoes are made from the reverse side, or back-side, of tree bark, not the white outer bark. The backside of the bark is prized for its cambium, the layer of soft growing tissue just beneath the inner bark. If the bark is harvested in winter, the cambium strongly adheres to the backside of the bark and creates a dark film, or canvas, upon which artisans can etch their unique designs and drawings into a canoe's surface. The canoe will have a brilliant, light golden glow if the bark is harvested in summer. Winter bark is more time consuming to harvest than spring- or summer-peeled bark and will considerably change the outward appearance of the canoe.

Canoeing at sunset on the Saranacs.

Elm bark can be used for siding in sheets comprised of just the bark or made into elm shingles where part of the tree's outer sapwood is cut in slabs with the bark left intact. The local Oneidas and Mohawks of the Iroquois Nation used elm bark to fully sheathe their longhouses, which were made of tree saplings bent for framing ribs, that housed their families. They also used elm bark for building canoes since the local birch did not always grow large enough.

The word *adirondack* is from the Algonquin word meaning "bark eater," aimed as an insult to their neighboring enemies, the Iroquois Nation, who navigated the rough, jagged terrain. It was also a term the Iroquois used to refer to the Algonquins, who were forced to live on tree bark during severe winters. It was common to see the bark from the birch trees stripped in patches for making baskets. Perhaps it was the small patches of birch bark missing from the trees that inspired the name.

The meaning of the term *adirondack* has been disputed often. J. B. Hewitt of the Smithsonian Institution believed it was derived from the language of a tribe of Indians who lived on the lower Saint Lawrence River in the early 1500s and meant "They of the Great Rocks." When it was passed on to the Iroquois, the meaning got jumbled to "They who eat trees."

Opposite: Bridges, planking, and log passages are used in this rugged terrain to create easier travel paths. Some camps don't have road access at all, and many lean-tos for overnight camping can be reached only by hiking or skiing miles into the wilderness. The bridge leads to Morningside Camps and Cabins in Minerva.

Adirondack Park

The untamed woods, rough terrain and rapid waters of Adirondack Park consist of approximately six million acres, nearly half of which belong to all the people of New York State and are constitutionally protected to remain "forever wild" forest preserve. The remaining half of the park is private land that includes settlements, farms, timberlands, businesses, homes, and camps.

Adirondack Park was created in 1892 by the State of New York amid concerns for the water and timber resources. Today it is the largest publicly protected area in the contiguous United States, greater in size than Yellowstone, Everglades, Glacier, and Grand Canyon National Parks combined. The park encompasses over 3,000 lakes, 30,000 miles of rivers and streams, and a wide variety of habitats,including globally unique wetland types and old-growth forests.

About 130,000 people live here year-round in just over a hundred towns and villages.

Spectacular scenery such as this massive waterfall rewards both beginning and experienced hikers.

Lean–tos

The Adirondack lean-to was developed by the New York State Conservation Department and Civilian Conservation Corps to house the working force that was part of a reforestation project. This design became the standard for lean-tos built on hiking trails developed during the 1920s and '30s throughout the state's Adirondack Forest Preserve.

Cross-country skiers taking a break at an Adirondack lean-to on the Jackrabbit Trail.

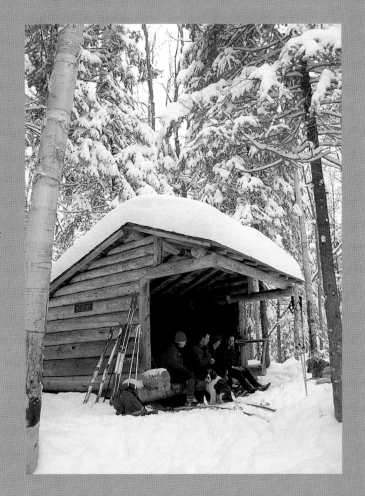

Architectural Details

The combination and use of natural materials collected and sculpted from the surrounding environment, such as elm and birch bark, twigs, tree saplings and large-diameter logs, are the basic components of Adirondack architecture. It is this combination and mix of materials, as well as the various textures, that bring a camp to life and create a one-of-a-kind sculptural form of architecture with undeniable distinction.

Vertical log columns are used as dividers and act as header supports that span the long distance of the picture window.

Adirondack Details

- Twig art, or free-form decorative "twig-onometry"
- Natural log railings or slat-board rails
- Adirondack siding
- Vertical log siding
- Bunk rooms that save space for hunting camps or family living
- Rustic furniture that blends with nature
- Window grille patterns and distinctive color choices within the window trim
- Shutters from plain to decorative—but always functional
- Fireplaces or wood stoves that more than just being aesthetic are also functional for heating and cooking
- Door styles and patterns that can be primitive or decorative
- Covered porches and sundecks to make the most of outdoor living

It is impossible for man-made objects to effectively compete with nature's wealth. Although, when one works with and not against nature, the final effect is warm, elegant and sculptural.

Porches, Patios and Decks

Adirondack camps have always featured and honored outdoor living, whether it's covered porches, sunlit patios or sun-drenched decks. Porches, in particular, have always been a large part of the architectural framework of an Adirondack camp. A room without walls can easily accommodate additional sleeping, reading or dining quarters, quickly becoming everyone's favorite room. After all, what would an Adirondack camp be without a porch?

Patios or decks are usually built onto the back or side of a home, creating a transition between the house and yard. Decks or patios lead easily into the gardenscape, weaving a natural tapestry. The terms *patio, deck* and *porch* are often used loosely and may be called various names from region to region. For example, a covered porch is called a portal in the Southwest, and a patio may be called a lanai or veranda in the Southeast.

Small twigs set in a free-form pattern hide the lapped joints of birch bark.

Opposite: Fan-backed Adirondack chairs silhouetted at sunrise.

PORCHES

The porch plays an important role in how a camp functions, feels and flows. These overhead roofs create added protection as the environment changes moods, from the direct heat of a sunny day to a summer's heavy rain. Although covered porches are best known for their grand entrances or as front-row seats to watch the world go by, they can be designed to enhance almost any side of a home.

In the right location, a porch can catch a summer breeze, soak in the sun's rays or be a platform for a panoramic view of nature. A porch

Opposite: Each camp is as individual as its owners, and every camp reflects their personality and style.

At the turn of the century, sleeping porches became popular for many reasons. Besides being comfortable on hot summer nights, they were doctor-recommended, as it was thought that sleeping out-of-doors would reduce the spread of contagious diseases such as tuberculosis.

can be a perfect spot to sip lemonade or enjoy a quiet cup of early morning tea as one watches the mist dissipate with the rising of the sun. A well-placed porch adds to the soul and spirit of any structure and can add symmetry or an architectural kick to the plainest of structures.

A covered porch on the south side of a home can dramatically cool the home from a summer's intense heat. On the east side, a porch could be a perfect spot for breakfast or contemplating the day ahead. Covered porches have their practical side, too. They greatly reduce the amount of maintenance on any home. Wide overhangs protect a home from the sun's harsh ultraviolet rays, constant water saturation and brutal winds.

In the Adirondacks, it has been the tradition to have a sleeping porch where one awakens to the view of a sparkling lake or listens at dusk to the call of the loon. At the turn of the twenty-first century, the Adirondacks served as an escape from the pollution and overcrowding of congested and noise-filled cities. It was considered a very important health benefit to be surrounded by fresh outdoor air and nature's calm. Today, these same benefits are treasured by many seeking refuge from the frantic pace of modern life.

An expansive porch can entertain large gatherings, yet also provide cozy spaces for intimate groupings. Often, porches can be transformed into outdoor dining rooms with front row seats to nature's own theater.

Twig art or free-form rails are labor-intensive to create. Every rail pattern is different and artists have their own individual style.

Yet too often, porches are overlooked and underestimated during the initial designing of a home. A carefully considered porch design can easily extend living space into the outdoors and create a balance to the house and property. With smart planning, most houses can gain an extra outdoor room, seamlessly connecting the interior to the outside.

Porches can easily be added to an existing camp. There are numerous styles of porches that can greatly enhance a home's appearance and value while also creating an inviting space. The addition of a porch can be subtle or it can be a dramatic change to an overall structure. In some cases, an add-on porch rather than a massive addition may be all that is needed to spruce up a drab and boring home.

This camp's exterior has a rustic mix of vertical log siding, open-spindle fretwork below the twig-art truss, and birch bark sheathing accenting the gable-end windows.

PATIOS AND DECKS

A deck or patio can also complement a home by imitating its architectural style and providing additional space for comfortable and cozy outdoor living. Although a standard wood deck is often the first choice, another nice backyard alternative is a patio that is usually made of stone, concrete or brick. Stone always improves with age and with exposure to nature's elements. Another benefit is that a stone or masonry patio absorbs the sun during the day and radiates its warmth longer into the night, creating its own microclimate. Stone hardscapes can be formal or informal, depending on the cut or texture of the natural stone. One thing to keep in mind is that stone is generally more expensive than a standard wood deck, but it is more upscale and durable, which may be a good investment if you plan to keep your home for a long period of time. Every cabin, cottage or camp should have a room without walls, whether it is a porch, patio or deck. After all, outdoor living is what camp life is all about!

Windows

Windows are an important component of a home's exterior and deserve extra attention to make them exciting. The right combination of color, style and size can make or break a cabin's appearance. Some builders choose recycled materials from older homes and barns to create their windows, breathing new life into a camp's design and functionality.

In today's market there are so many styles, colors and patterns of window grilles and frames. The Adirondack-style window features

This door cleverly blends color and texture at the Santanoni Camp. The mix of hand-peeled saplings with ones that have the bark left on creates texture and depth.

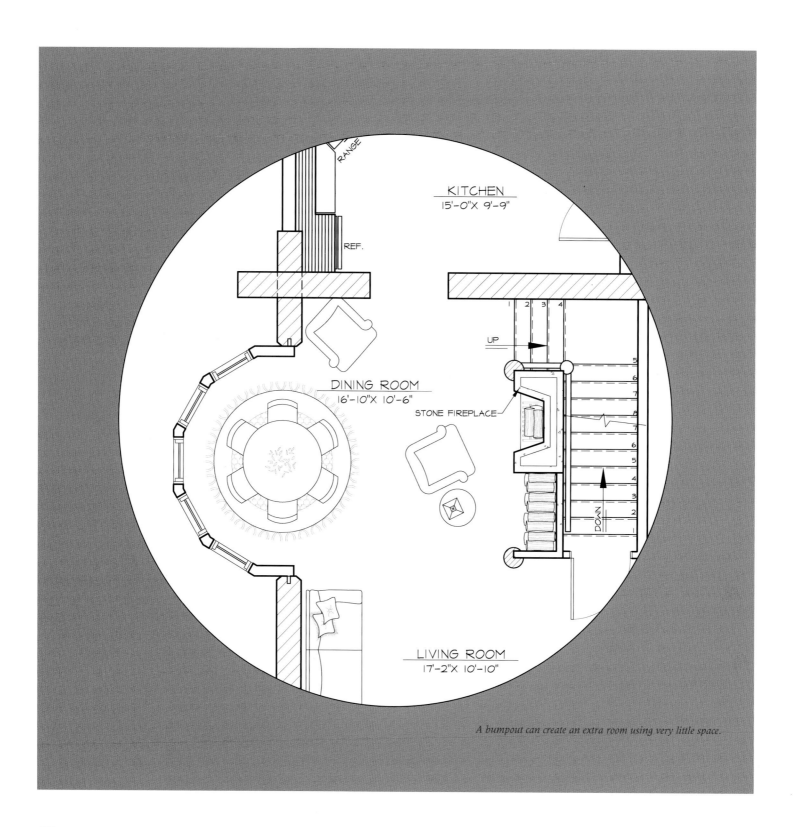

KITCHEN
15'-0"X 9'-9"

RANGE

REF.

DINING ROOM
16'-10"X 10'-6"

STONE FIREPLACE

UP

DOWN

LIVING ROOM
17'-2"X 10'-10"

A bumpout can create an extra room using very little space.

a diverse combination of vibrant colors such as the famous Adirondack greens, cranberry reds, turquoise blues, shades of subtle browns and butter yellows.

Using a wide trim to frame a window is a secret design detail that gives a more traditional look to any home. Take a look at older homes in your neighborhood and you will notice that all the old window trims are 4 to 6 inches wide. Then look at a newly built home and notice that it has little or no trim surrounding the window. A window without a wide trim can look like eyes without eyebrows. This is a subtle detail that can greatly change the appearance of a home.

Positioning a cabin, camp or cottage to take advantage of the best view is not as easy as it looks. Many aspects must work together, such as design, excavation and construction.

Window Seats

The aesthetic qualities of window seats should not be overlooked; window seats are fun, elegant and can be very affordable. They are great places to sit and dream—ideal for people and pets. They make good use of limited space, expanding a room's feel and function. They can be made very simple and at little cost, or they can be extravagant in style, expense and detail.

A bay or bow window can create a great sunroom effect for plants and herbs, a bench for extra seating or can be used as alcove seating or a dining nook for a less formal, more intimate eating area. No matter how you do it, the window seat will wrap you in nature and light. A bay window can seem to add a whole room. It can be a great way to create an eat-in kitchen without having to build extra space. (See example on page 52.)

Railings and Twig Art

The Adirondacks are famous for free-form railings, slat-board rails and twig art. These branches and twigs may be collected on hiking trips or from your backyard. Some artisans labor full-time with this very difficult medium, contorting the twigs into flowing sculptures that gracefully ornament a structure to give an Adirondack camp its distinctive look and feel. The twig art may appear simple to create, but in reality it is very labor-intensive and time-consuming to achieve. Adirondack free-form rail-

ings are created using twigs and branches and can be quite expensive or surprisingly affordable, depending on the labor involved and whether the design is elaborate. Railings can be a focal point of the Adirondack architecture of a camp, blending in with the overall design or functioning strictly as utilitarian. (See example on page 56.)

Many Adirondack camps have open-framed, uninsulated walls. These wall cavities are used in many ways; here the wall cavities hold the camp owner's library. Extra beds are tucked into the living area's corner. The ceiling framing is also left exposed to keep the cost of construction to a minimum.

Adirondack-style rustic furniture and an elaborate handcrafted twig bed enhance this suite overlooking the water at the Mirror Lake Inn.

Inset: The "twig-onometry" of free-form work is accented by a carved squirrel.

SLAT BOARD RAILS

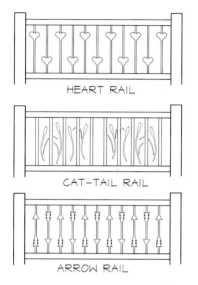

HEART RAIL

CAT-TAIL RAIL

ARROW RAIL

LOG & TWIG RAILS

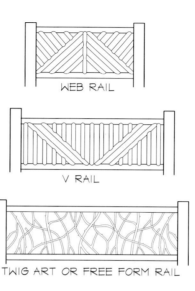

WEB RAIL

V RAIL

TWIG ART OR FREE FORM RAIL

At left are a few varieties of slat railings. The patterns created can be as unique as their creator. Slat rails can add more privacy to a loft than its more traditional spindle cousins.

Above right are just a few examples of log spindles and free-form railing patterns. The log variations can be tedious to create, yet just a small section mixed in with straight rails can really create a fantastic visual impact.

Every Adirondack camp must have its character piece. A forked newel is used at the base of the stairs and adds nature's own whimsy to the hallway of Placid Manor.

Doors

The style of a door can capture the rustic charm of a camp or cabin. An entry door can set the tone for an entire dwelling and greatly influence its overall appearance. Traditionally, Adirondack camp doors were made from items scavenged from the land, created from scratch by a local sawyer or handcrafted on-site. Another popular choice in many of the older camps was to use recycled doors to distinguish the camp entry. Doors can be fashioned out of irregular wood planks or standard dimensional lumber, or they can be embellished with tree saplings and twigs. There are many options on the market from stock doors to custom creations. They run the gamut from bead board and rustic wanes board to craftsman forms of Arts and Crafts style, to name only a few.

Near upper Saranac Lake. The small-diameter outrigger beams are doubled up and supported by knee braces that hold the entry roof system.

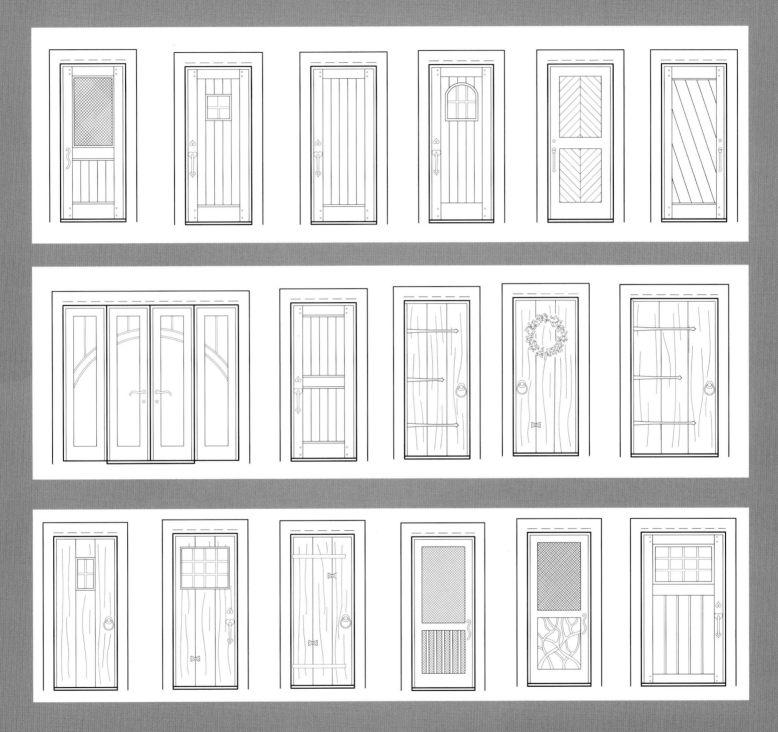

Adding a certain style of door can bring a very different
feel to a home's design. Selecting just the right one can add
greatly to a cabin's charm and appeal.

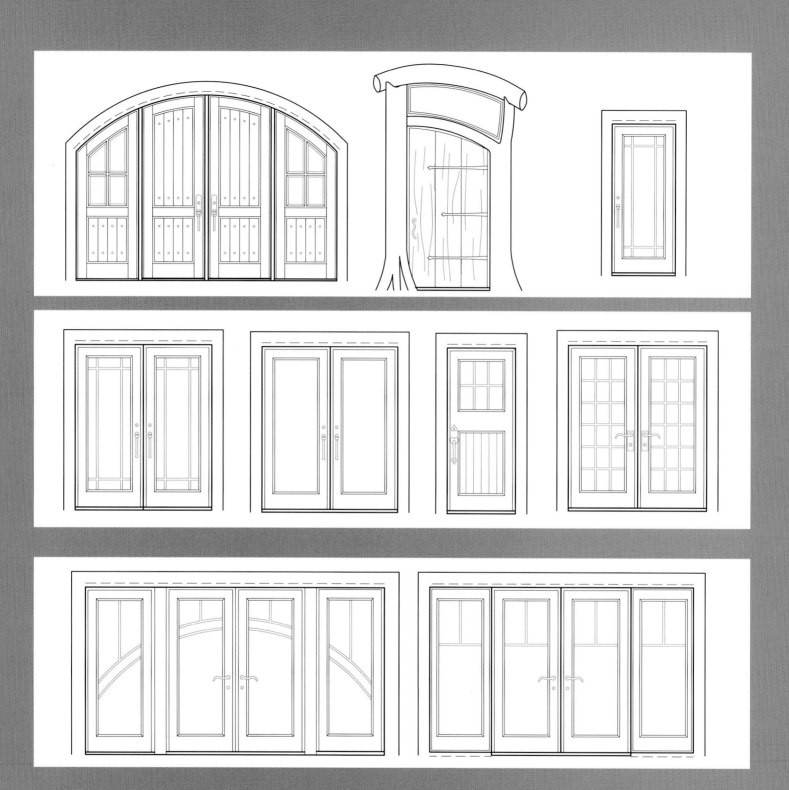

Doors and entry trim can add drama to a home's exterior. Some might match other exterior elements, such as shutters or trim, while others stand alone in splendid prominence.

Shutter designs can be a solid color, two-toned, or many colors combined.

Shutters

Shutters protect camps from storms and break-ins by animals such as bears or raccoons. They not only add security but make a window appear bigger and more prominent. More than functional, shutters can become an added architectural element or accent. They also give the opportunity to work another accent color into the trim. Some craftsmen create and insert an ornamental function or a signature style within their shutters. Maple leaf, pine tree, fish, bird, moose, and flower cutouts or wood, metal, or painted inlays show the creative signatures of these craftsmen. Options are endless and limited only by one's imagination.

Bunk Rooms

Few of us have the money or time to spend on large estates with full-time summer staffs of gardeners, cooks, housekeepers and nannies. As a result, today's Adirondack great camps are typically small and more practical in structure. Bunk rooms offer a space-saving design element as they can provide sleeping quarters with many beds, depending upon need. Some camps have the luxury of two bunk rooms, separating quarters for men and women. The bunk room is a concept that never lost its allure due to its flexible and practical use.

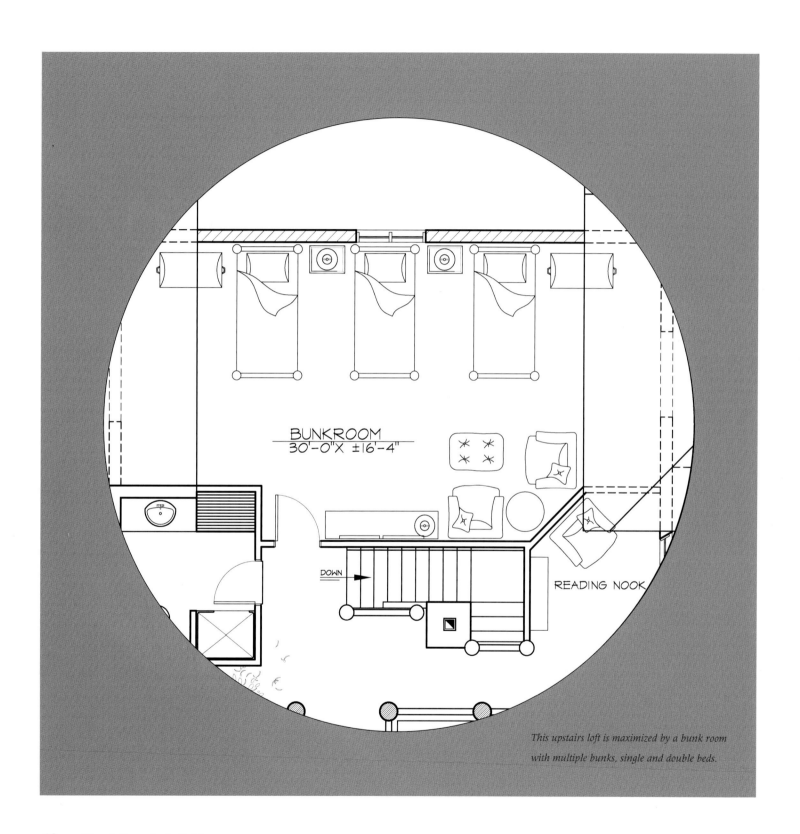

BUNKROOM
30'-0"X ±16'-4"

DOWN

READING NOOK

*This upstairs loft is maximized by a bunk room
with multiple bunks, single and double beds.*

We are still designing homes with bunk rooms, and they are regaining popularity because of their simplicity and cost efficiency.

Outdoor Showers

There is nothing better than an outdoor shower, and it's making a popular comeback. Once the proportions and size are right, where the shower is not too tall, too large or small, then you will have a shower that would satisfy even Goldilocks' finicky taste.

You must consider the shower's location for privacy and convenience to the home. If the shower walls or roof are too large, the shower room can engulf the camp and make the proportions out of balance. The use of an overhead roof is not necessary, but with short summers, a roof helps retain the heat of shower steam.

Attention to detail is important; a comfortable bench at the right height is nice for sitting to remove shoes and clothes, store extra supplies or elevate your belongings so they do not become wet. Adding a shelf to place shampoos, soaps and razors is helpful. Think about areas where you can place pegs for hand towels, robes and clothes, and additional guest hooks for wet bathing suits out of the way of shower mist; also consider drainage and decking so you are not standing in mud or sand.

One home had a freestanding shower not attached to the home yet convenient to the home's entry. The boards were offset at the joints, allowing good ventilation and southern light through a wooden shutter on a pulley that could be pulled open from the inside. The port-style window was high enough to still be very private. Outdoor showers can be the ultimate garden room, freeing up the bathroom, especially in a one-bath camp.

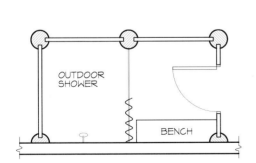 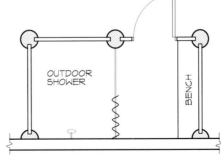 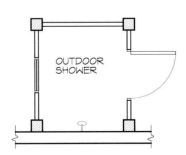

An outdoor shower is a great addition to any camp. It can free up an already overcrowded bathroom.

Fireplaces and Wood Stoves

A fireplace appeals to many of our senses: one feels the heat, smells the log's sweet sap, hears the hissing and cracking of the fire, and sees the calming flicker of the fire's flame. The strobing flame draws us into a hypnotic and tranquil state of mind. Used for heating and cooking, the fireplace or wood stove is a functional and aesthetic part of the architecture. In the Adirondack Mountains, a fire may even have to be started in June to take the nip out of the early morning air. Short Adirondack summers, however, may call for outdoor kitchens. Sheltered under a lean-to or shed roof, a wood stove keeps the heat out of a camp and allows you to enjoy and spend more time outdoors.

The large-diameter log parlins span the weight of the roof, then exit through the vertical-log-sided gable, where their bark is left intact.

Left: The combination of living room, dining room and kitchen create a casual feel at the heart of this camp.

Below: This room at Lake Placid Lodge offers both a cozy fireplace and an unforgettable view.

Right: Most Adirondack camps have names, and this one is known as Hermit's Hut. The asymmetrical fireplace adds whimsy to this room, and large timber accents of bead board ceilings add texture and depth to this charming cabin.

Inset: A glimpse of the great room at Garnet Hill Lodge in North River.

Furniture

The Adirondacks are known for their hearty craftspeople who, with creativity and ingenuity, learned to work with Mother Nature. The rustic furniture of the classic Adirondack camps was originally fashioned by these resourceful caretakers as they shaped and carved the trunks, bark and branches of local trees into usable furnishings. Though utility was the purpose, artistry was the result. These artisans continue to build and create heirlooms for the future. However, even without distinctive Adirondack furnishings, today's great camps may be enhanced by natural elements, garage sale finds and leftover furnishings. A mix of junkyard discoveries can create an eclectic look that makes the camp seem less stiff and formal.

Top: This bark-on furniture echoes the log walls. The horizontal logs show a chinked lateral groove between the log courses.

Above: This cherry red Adirondack chair is a wonderful accent to the white birch with yellow fall color.

*Top: A mix of textures, colors and patterns
create added depth and warmth in a room.
The walls themselves are created with a pattern of vertical and horizontal log saplings.*

*A birch bark–sheathed bed and bench
created by Larry Hawkins, in St. Regis Suite
at Lake Placid Lodge.*

*Above: Visitors can curl up to read a book
at the library in Mirror Lake Inn.*

*Lake Placid Lodge is well known in the
Adirondacks for its comfortable rooms and
cabins, five-star food, and extensive wine
cellar. Note the use of birch bark within
the papered ceiling. The decorative twig
patterns actually hide the joints of the
bark and hold them in place.*

Log and Timber Trusses

When building a structure with log elements, you can use a single truss as an accent or you can stack a room with many trusses. Depending on a home's design, the use of a single truss may be all that is needed, while another room may benefit architecturally by the use of a team of trusses.

Besides truss style, there are many things that can make a truss look different. The species of wood, such as white pine verses a western fire-kill timber, or the use of reclaimed logs or timbers can drastically change the appearance of the wood's surface patina. A truss will also look very different depending on the craftsman's skills and joinery techniques and application or combinations.

The choice of wood can also affect the structural integrity of a home. For example, cedar and white pine

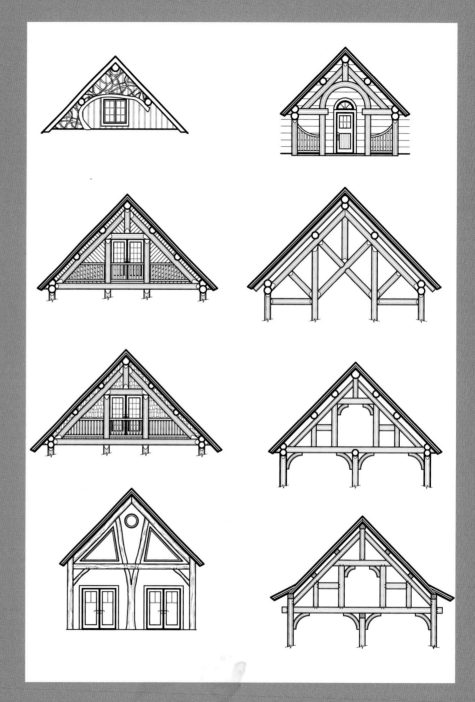

Trusses and purlins can use full round logs, square logs or a combination of both. The use of timber accents or log elements can drastically change the appearance of the home's design.

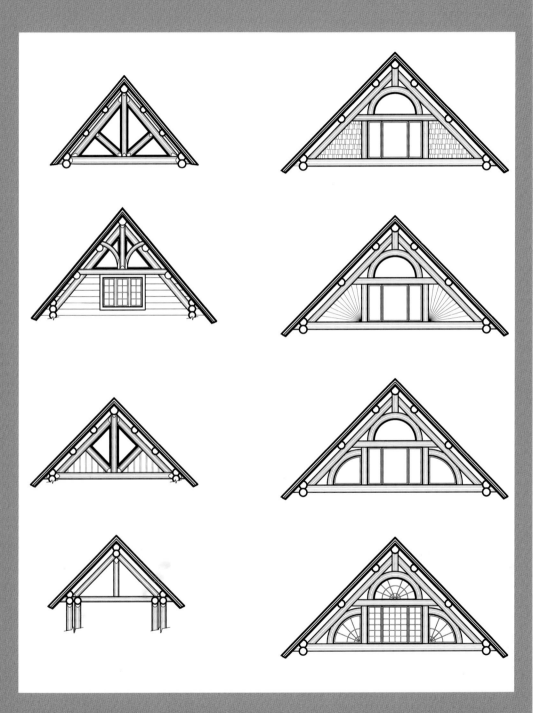

Gable end trusses and purlins can be used in different combinations to achieve a myriad of exterior facades. The log accents can be structural or decorative, but be sure to have a whole timber specialist help with the viability of the actual struc-tural integrity. So many mistakes are made by those who don't understand the properties of whole log construction.

are not structural woods for long spanning distances, yet with small spans or the use of structural supporting columns, this indigenous wood of the Adirondacks works tremendously well. The added characteristic of white pine and cedar is that they have minimal spiral grain, less shrinkage and are easy to carve. Although white pine and cedar are usually a craftsman's preferred woods, they also have a tendency to blue stain. This is only the tip of the yin and yang of complexities of wood's characteristics. Every wood has its advantages and disadvantages; it is experience and an understanding of how to work with different species of wood that make a better, more informed builder. It is truly the combination of many factors that creates the perfect truss; it is when a builder learns to work with a wood's natural properties that the art of a true craftsman is obtained.

Also note that not every truss will work in all locations. Some truss styles are more decorative and not as structural in the design itself. Roof, snow and wind loads will affect trusses differently. Just because you love a truss design does not make it work in all situations and applications. It takes years to learn the trade and the complexities of truss building. It is a complicated process that takes great knowledge to create even a simple truss. A typical conventional 2 x 6 framer or builder isn't likely to have the added skill or experience necessary to engineer a log or timber truss that stands the test of time. Also, a novice builder may not consider that adding a heavy log or timber and attaching or bolting the timber to the bottom of a roof's framing can add considerable point loads or extra inverted dead loads to the roofline that will flex the roof system over time.

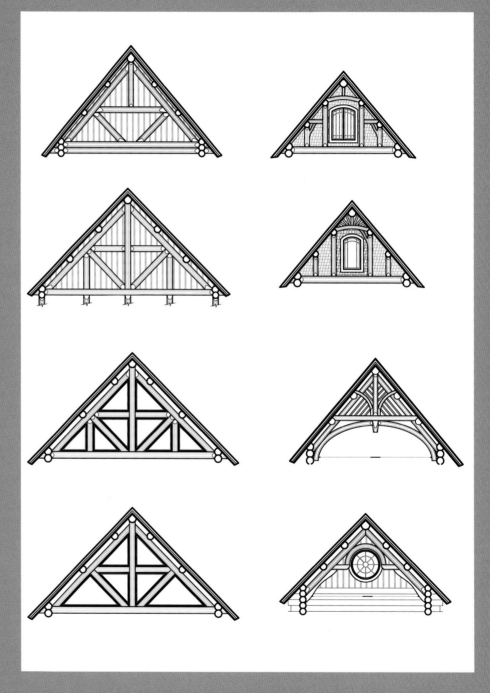

The material you choose for sheathing behind or between trusses can change the appearance of the home's exterior. Such depth can be created by the choice of materials. Some of the voids can be filled with glass or framed and shielded with boards, shingles, or bark.

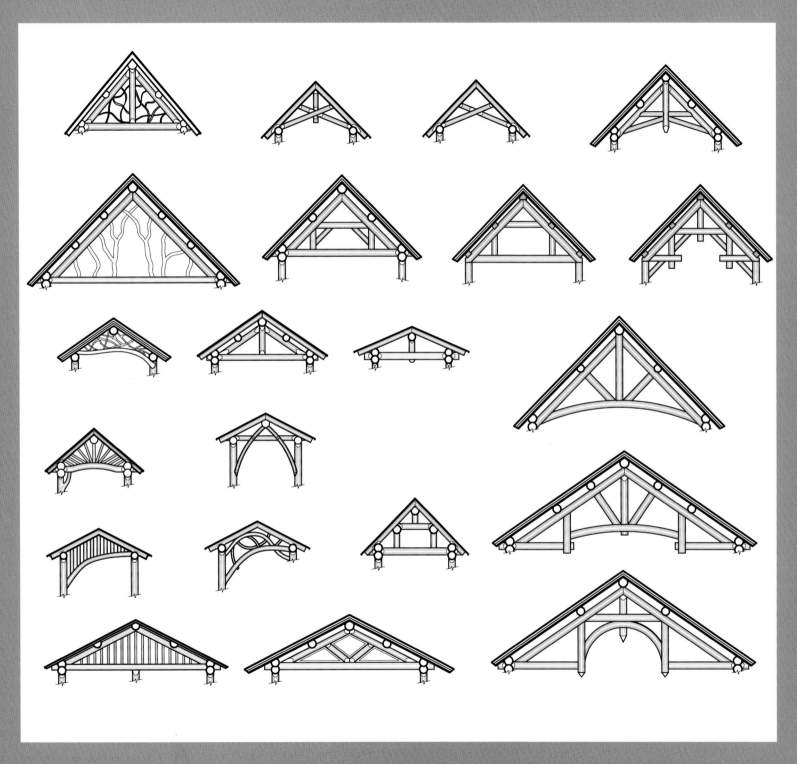

Each truss has its own character. Trusses can be minimal in appearance or complex in design. They can be whimsical or tailored and formal.

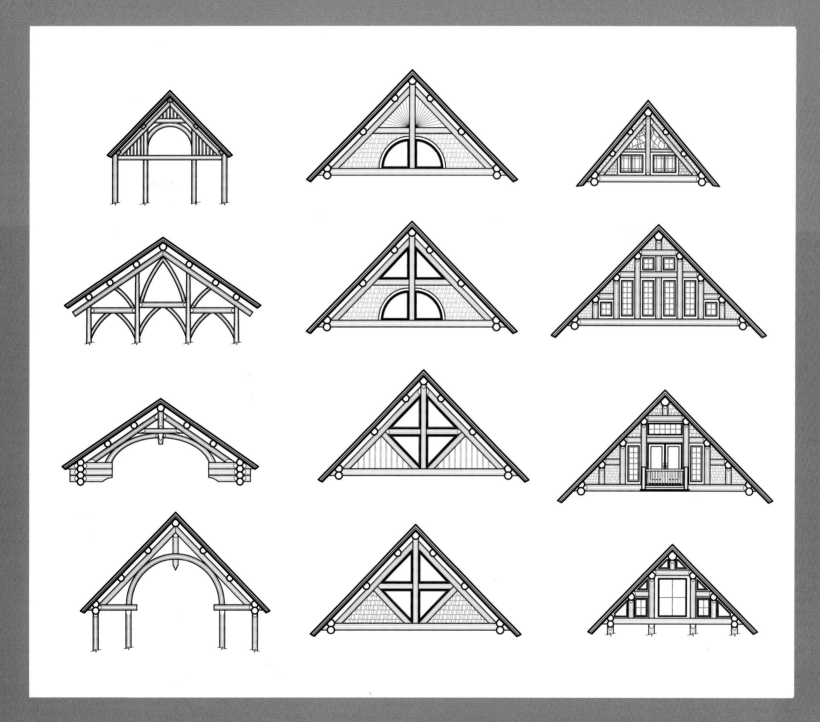

The four trusses in the left column are entry or interior center trusses. The remaining two columns are gable-end truss configurations. Notice that the four trusses in the center column and the four trusses in the right column are the same, but the look changes based on the different window shapes, sheathing applications, and doors.

The Craftspeople

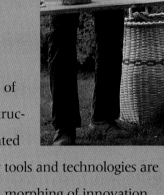

Log-element construction is typically used to create a conventionally built structure that uses log elements as either structural supports or merely decorative accents. This creates an extremely customized style of building that is not conducive to manufactured mass-production techniques.

Log-element construction is a trade that appears simple to those who have not experienced the reality of this form of construction. It is one of the few businesses where customers and passers-by with no experience offer to help an experienced tradesperson simplify a project. Log-element construction appears to be straightforward and a matter of common sense; however, the interfacing of countless and varied components makes the process much more complex and time-consuming than assumed.

Handcrafters are skilled individuals who have a passion for working with wood and nature. Most joinery techniques are passed down through many generations. Other techniques are developed out of necessity from recycled structures left behind or invented by creative minds as new tools and technologies are being developed. It is this morphing of innovation, technology and creativity that breeds a new hybrid of distinctive log-element architecture and passionate artisans. Log-element hybrids are influenced by regional styles and structural features that inspire new construction techniques.

Architecture can be transformed and influenced through many factors, such as economics, life experience, environment and pop culture. A log-element structure is going to look very different in the Adirondacks than in the Southeast, Southwest or Northwest. Although the components and joinery are very similar, it is regional influences, indigenous materials and local application that greatly affect the overall appearance.

Small Gems

Considering a smaller footprint for a home brings surprising rewards. The construction of smaller camps, cottages and cabins uses fewer resources to construct and maintain, therefore gaining more home benefits for less cost. A kitchenette or apartment-style galley not only offers a big break in cost (since kitchens and baths are the largest ticket items of any home) but also forces preparation of a simpler meal along with the added bonus of a quicker clean-up. Do not fear—with some ingenuity you

The walls of this log cabin are constructed in the chink style with mortar between courses of logs. The gable-end walls that fill in the ends of the log cabin are sheathed in vertical log siding. The mix of fabrics and rustic mountain furniture work together to create the warmth and romance of the Adirondack style.

can still create gourmet foods in a smaller kitchen.

The simple four-corner structures are often what we imagine when we think of cabin life and vacation homes. With a smaller structure we can have more time to enjoy the outdoors, using that as our extended living room. It is that infectious disease of cabin fever we all hope to catch.

There is nothing that captures the heart or exudes the romance of camp life more than the charm and simplicity of a small camp. Often we stray from a small footprint because it seems so small on paper, or our eyes become larger than our pocketbooks, or we forget that to

A sleeping room has a fireplace flanked by birch saplings. The header of the fire pit is made with a hand-hewn timber. Simple, natural accents add character.

Opposite: With limited space and experienced planning, this pantry is creatively tucked under the slope of the stairs. The simplicity of the cabinet design creates a clean look. Some Adirondack camps tend toward the simple lines of the Shaker style, while others display a more Victorian ornamentation. Still others are a mix of styles—Mission, Craftsman, European, Native American, or Asian. It is this eclectic mix that becomes the Adirondack style.

really enjoy nature we may only need something as minimal as the size of a standard hotel room, like in a one-room cabin. The idea of enjoying nature is to minimize your surroundings.

My favorite camps and cabins are only 20 x 30 feet, all on one floor, with low-pitch rooflines that blend into the surroundings. You can arrange the plan to fit one or two bedrooms or create a ladder to a

space that is good for storage or extra mattresses. Creativity is pushed when you are limited to a certain size, but it can make the best project.

Space-Saving Ideas

- Using only one bathroom per home or minimizing the number of bathrooms will save on space and money as well as lessen everyone's least favorite chore—the dreaded cleaning.

- Building the bedrooms smaller than the other rooms may be a considered choice since many of us spend most of our time in that room with our eyes shut.
- Bunk rooms can minimize square-foot consumption by having two to three sets of bunk beds in one room.
- Smaller and simpler camp-style kitchens or the use of outdoor/ summer kitchens greatly reduce construction costs.
- An outdoor shower can free up the home's bathrooms and when designed properly can be very comfortable.
- Organized and efficient use of closets can greatly maximize a home's limited square footage.

Ten Ways to Make a Small Camp Feel Large

1. Use a stacked washer and dryer to free some space for added storage of linens or utilities.

2. Use dormers or a shed roof in a sloped ceiling area. Dormers will add headroom as well as more interesting details to the overall architecture. Keep in mind that bump-outs and dormers add significantly to construction materials, time and price.

3. Take advantage of the space within knee walls. You can reclaim closet space by creating a built-in dresser; low closets for seasonal storage; mechanical storage for plumbing, electricity and

This outhouse is sided with vertical log siding made of cedar saplings.

Opposite: Simple materials like fall leaves accent a camp and provide natural décor year-round.

heating; a front-load washer and dryer; or built-in bookshelves.

4. Add a bay window to create a greenhouse for herbs, a comfortable window seat or a cozy reading nook.

5. Add a pantry to triple the amount of space for dry goods and storage.

6. Utilize the basement. Spend more time planning the use of this often-forgotten space, as it is the least expensive space to develop. With extra effort the basement does not have to be dark, damp or dingy. Large plates of patio doors and over-sized windows can help elevate a basement tremendously. If you don't want the cost of extra-deep frost walls, then choose to place windows higher up than the ground level so a great deal of daylight can be captured. Windows strategically

The colors of fall drape a small camp, allowing the low horizontal structure to blend perfectly into the landscape.

placed higher can still flood the basement with light.

7. Control the accumulation of belongings with clever closet organization, kitchen and bath planning, and by microanalyzing every inch of space. Decluttering a home draws attention to the beauty of the home and not to the confusion of items in disarray. Organization is key. There are so many charities and organizations that could make use of extra stuff.

8. Add a porch to your home's design. Porches are finally in the spotlight they deserve. Americans everywhere are celebrating the original porches of colonial times. It wasn't until the 1940s or '50s when we started to modernize and streamline our homes, eliminating porches from the design. Porches make a house look larger than it really is. One drawback to a smaller home is less space to entertain, so a porch provides the perfect spot for social gatherings of family and friends, regardless of the home's size.

9. Find a lighting specialist. Lighting is more than windows and lamps. A professional in lighting can make the most of your home, but don't overdo it! When log walls become riddled with plugs, switches, sconces and window cutouts, the walls are no longer showcased. They become cluttered and appear choppy. On the other hand, many homes have inadequate lighting. Log walls and camp-style homes tend to be darker in tone and reflect less light than their Sheetrock cousins. The keys are balance, proportion and planning.

10. Hire good design professionals—this is a small part of a home's overall cost. It is not only the design professional's experience but also their compatibility with the client that matters. It is important to like the design professional's style; some have a traditional or old-world style while others may have a modern or contemporary approach. A good designer can bring a whole new level of artistry, experience and quality to a structure's design. The art of planning and design is the secret to creating a home that feels larger as well as more comfortable, practical and functional. A good design will create flow and better proportions within any structure.

A handcrafted outdoor gazebo creates some overhead shelter from the elements. The use of log and twig elements or accents is part of the Adirondack charm.

Good
Design

Although the Adirondacks have a distinctive ruggedness, an Adirondack-style camp is not cluttered or boring and does not appear to have been hit with the ugly stick. Ironically, it takes an enormous amount of planning to achieve simplicity and attractiveness. The more planning you do before construction, the easier actual construction becomes since most of the guesswork can be eliminated. Ideas and strategies can evolve over many years; it can take what seems like an eternity to properly plan and research in order to create your dream. Through the

The doorways are accented and framed by log saplings, creating a simple elegance. Yet the simplicity is an illusion, as a skilled craftsman must use every ounce of skill and infuse each piece with passion and soul to achieve the desired result.

Opposite: The owner's collection of books, art and old furniture are artistically placed to complement the glimpses of nature through the oversized windows. The keys to Adirondack design are the asymmetrical placement of furnishings as well as successful mixing of the old with the new and the natural pieces with manufactured objects.

Below: A step back in time to one of Otis Mountain Camp's kitchens. The walls are open-framed and whitewashed. The wall cavities are used for necessary storage.

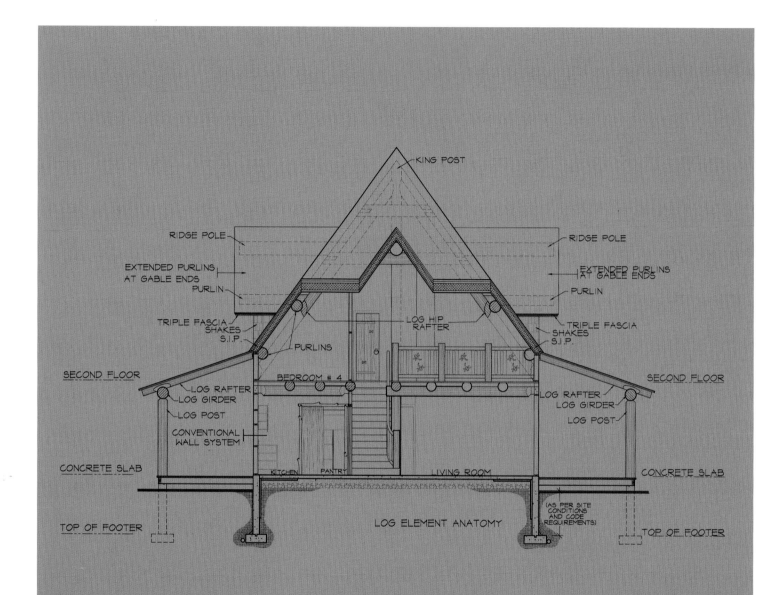

KING POST

RIDGE POLE

RIDGE POLE

EXTENDED PURLINS
AT GABLE ENDS

EXTENDED PURLINS
AT GABLE ENDS

PURLIN

PURLIN

LOG HIP
RAFTER

TRIPLE FASCIA
SHAKES
S.I.P.

TRIPLE FASCIA
SHAKES
S.I.P.

PURLINS

SECOND FLOOR

SECOND FLOOR

BEDROOM # 4

LOG RAFTER
LOG GIRDER

LOG RAFTER
LOG GIRDER

LOG POST

LOG POST

CONVENTIONAL
WALL SYSTEM

CONCRETE SLAB

KITCHEN   PANTRY   LIVING ROOM

CONCRETE SLAB

TOP OF FOOTER

LOG ELEMENT ANATOMY

(AS PER SITE
CONDITIONS
AND CODE
REQUIREMENTS)

TOP OF FOOTER

*Log elements are not log walls, but a conventionally built structure with log
accents such as log floor joists, log stairs, log roof and rafter supports, and
railings. Log elements can be minimal or complex, depending on the design.*
*The contrast of these elements can create great rustic accents that tie the
architecture to the outdoors. (Cross section of Camp Dragonfly on page 112) .*

LOG ELEMENT ANATOMY

process of good design you can develop a sense of movement that brings a home to life. The Adirondack style can be funky, whimsical or traditional with improvisational flair. The Adirondack craftsman's elements and accents are not a McLog type of construction where quick, inexpensive methods or modular forms are used.

It is during the design stage when you plan and record your wishes and needs on paper so your dream can be represented in a cohesive fashion, translated into the codes and requirements of the builder and subtrades. It is this added time that creates a camp that focuses on an attention to details. This attention early in the process will create a cohesive vision that will translate into a visual reward.

With seasonal camps that have limited space, every wall cavity is put to use.

An experienced design professional can help you keep your dream in line with your budget, although there are many factors that can alter the cost of even the smallest structures. Planning helps you work through the different stages of construction with its limitless choices and complex issues. It takes time to develop a plan from scratch. A simple preliminary drawing can be developed quickly, but it is the construction details that take time to develop so the trades don't have to spend as much time on-site reconfiguring how to make the project work.

The conventional rafters are left exposed, revealing the structural framing. The diamond grilles of the windows were typical in many of the Adirondack camps at the turn of the century. The patchwork of the quilt complements the headboard sheathed in birch bark.

There will always be things the
trades must do on-site, but more
detail and planning ahead of time
will make a job site much more
efficient as well as more artistic. It
takes time, effort and experience to
create a structure that blends in
with nature and its surroundings.

Not every home design will fit a
property. Design is not only about
the interiors; extra time and planning are needed to be sure the
home fits to the slope of the land,
the neighboring structures and
the natural water runoff that may
not be visible on a typical sunny
day. Every homeowner should
invest the time necessary to make
their cabin comfortable, warm
and inviting.

*Combining the living room, dining room and kitchen
into one common room promotes togetherness while
also simplifying the structure's cost and complexities.*

The Importance of Proper Engineering

Construction knowledge requires years of practical on-site experience to learn the lessons of building far beyond what you could learn from a construction program on television or read from a book or magazine.

Something about building a rustic camp exudes romance. There is a bit of homesteading genetically wired in many of us. We romanticize about the cabin in the woods or the camp nestled along a crisp, clear lakeshore. But the reality

On the left rests a traditional birch-bark canoe with spruce roots used to tie and secure the ribs to the top frame. An Adirondack guide boat, at right, offers yet another form of silent transportation.

is just because one has a bit of woodchuck in one's soul does not mean that mistakes or building challenges will not arise.

History has seen passionate people whose wonderful dreams turned into nightmares because they built without proper engineering. Even within the industry there are improper engineering practices and inadequate or corner-cutting methods used. Whether you build a home out of stone, brick, stucco or wood, following proper engineering practices will ensure that your thoughtful design results in a beautiful home.

Engineers, architects and specialized design consultants are underused and underappreciated. The dynamics of whole-log construction methods are unique and

The asymmetry present in the fireplace and upper window creates a playful design, proving that straight and square isn't always best.

A glimpse into a three-sided Adirondack lean-to shows the framework of the structure; here weight loads and point loads are transferred at strategic points.

A group of kids enjoy an Adirondack lean-to camping adventure.

unlike other building methods. You would be surprised at how inexpensive it is to hire any one of these professionals to review plans and drawings and to work with your builder throughout the process of building. It is most certainly the least expensive route if problems occur down the road that require major repairs that could have otherwise been avoided.

With a bit more attention to properly engineering a log home or log-element structure, a home can be obtained that will not spread or creep over time. Building a home with large logs or timbers that appear straight today does not mean they will remain that way. Most structural failures don't reveal themselves until years after construction. Knowing and understanding these specialized trade standards can save money and many headaches in the long run.

This great room allows for large gatherings or quiet conversation, with the massive stone fireplace as the focal point. The gable end is lined with windows to naturally light the room.

Using Stock Plans

Purchasing stock plans is an economical way to design and build a home. Keep in mind that even these plans may need to be adjusted or customized based on weather conditions, local code requirements, regional site conditions, and type, size and product specifications, let alone your family's personal needs.

Quality illustrations of plans will reduce the risk of oversights, overspending and miscommunication between the trades. Accurate plans, better illustrations and clearer home specifications greatly reduce the amount of project delays and mistakes made on-site. Providing clear, accurate information will help the numerous suppliers and subtrades better understand your needs, dreams and goals.

Log Building Myths

There have been many log home building myths that have taken on a life of their own. Often these myths are created by poor workmanship or uninformed builders and homeowners who are not trained in the specialized medium. Here are some of the most common myths.

- *Vaulted ceilings are more homey.* Truth: Vaulted ceilings do not always create a sense of comfort and security. They're great for photos, but as a general rule they can also make a room lose its coziness. Even though they are currently all the rage, vaulted ceilings should be used sparingly.
- *Heating bills are higher with log homes.* Truth: A quality-built log

Split-cedar saplings with retained outer bark are laid on the diagonals to create a pattern of texture, making a focal point for the main entry door. The owners designed the door and stained glass art, choosing the bear and wolf motifs to reflect their affinity for the magnificent animals.

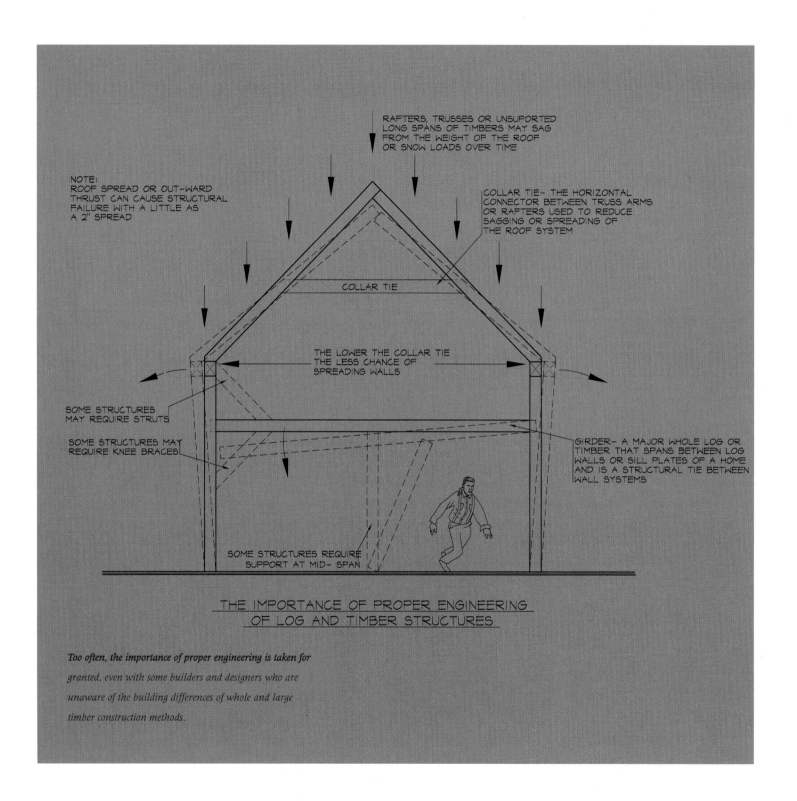

RAFTERS, TRUSSES OR UNSUPORTED
LONG SPANS OF TIMBERS MAY SAG
FROM THE WEIGHT OF THE ROOF
OR SNOW LOADS OVER TIME

NOTE:
ROOF SPREAD OR OUT-WARD
THRUST CAN CAUSE STRUCTURAL
FAILURE WITH A LITTLE AS
A 2" SPREAD

COLLAR TIE- THE HORIZONTAL
CONNECTOR BETWEEN TRUSS ARMS
OR RAFTERS USED TO REDUCE
SAGGING OR SPREADING OF
THE ROOF SYSTEM

COLLAR TIE

THE LOWER THE COLLAR TIE
THE LESS CHANCE OF
SPREADING WALLS

SOME STRUCTURES
MAY REQUIRE STRUTS

SOME STRUCTURES MAY
REQUIRE KNEE BRACES

GIRDER- A MAJOR WHOLE LOG OR
TIMBER THAT SPANS BETWEEN LOG
WALLS OR SILL PLATES OF A HOME
AND IS A STRUCTURAL TIE BETWEEN
WALL SYSTEMS

SOME STRUCTURES REQUIRE
SUPPORT AT MID- SPAN

THE IMPORTANCE OF PROPER ENGINEERING
OF LOG AND TIMBER STRUCTURES

Too often, the importance of proper engineering is taken for granted, even with some builders and designers who are unaware of the building differences of whole and large timber construction methods.

home is generally warmer than a conventionally built home. Only if it is not built properly will the home be colder. Poor quality includes these culprits: the diameter of the log walls are not thick enough; the log joinery is inferior; the carpenters did not respect or follow the shrinkage detail, which creates wall hang-ups; too many windows are used; there are too many vaulted areas and fireplace drafts.

- *A small home is a cheap home.* Truth: Quality costs more, regardless of the size of a home. Many people trade their original dream of a large home for one with a smaller footprint in order to ensure that they may have superior quality and beauty in a home that will endure.

Porches, decks and patios are important design features of any Adirondack camp.

- *Logs must be kiln dried in all log homes.* Truth: Most handcrafted log homes have been built with green logs (95 percent or more are not kiln dried). The most sophisticated joinery techniques and quality handcrafted log homes are built with green logs. It is this phobia of shrinkage along with marketing tactics that have created fear in the unknowing client. It does matter if you have 1 inch or 8 inches of shrinkage. This is all a natural part of handcrafted construction, and if you and your builder are aware of this very natural process, it is very simple to control. Settling is only a problem if you do not allow for it. The design detail of shrinkage is not hard or complicated for an experienced carpenter; it only becomes difficult when ignored.

- *A small structure does not need to be engineered.* Truth: Even the smallest of homes needs someone with experience to review the structure. Some houses end up having logs that span distances that are just too far without supports. This is a problem not readily seen until years later after the weight of the log has bowed the roofline over time. Other houses may have logs with mortise and tenons that are cut too small for the placement or span. Or the mortise and tenons are cut too large out of the support below or over the top of a window or door header. This can cause oversized stress cracks or bind the window and door openings. Also, the weight of a log adds a dead load to the roof or wall below that may not be expected by a novice builder.

- *Drying out logs quickly is good for the log shell.* Truth: It is better to slowly dry the logs over many years, as drying too quickly can cause the logs to develop large checks that trap water when located on the upper surfaces of the logs' exteriors. Some log species naturally check more than others, and there are ways to help draw the checks to the lateral grooves by making what is called a kerf cut into the logs' upper and lower lateral grooves, where they cannot be seen. There are also anti-check applications that can be applied to the logs' surfaces, helping to retard excessive checking.

Adirondack great camps of today can provide an individual or family of any size, income or lifestyle with a refreshing alternative to city, or even country, living. With

The old 20 x 20-foot cabins at Lake Placid Lodge are the perfect size for vacation camps. Cabins do not have to be large to be wrapped in luxury.

Opposite: Simple but elegant baths are part of Adirondack décor.

a little ingenuity and determination, anyone can develop a uniquely personalized camp that is comfortable and cozy. It is the combination of the dream, imagination and reality that will create your perfect Adirondack great camp.

Adirondack Plans

Indian Lake

The classic Adirondack camp with plenty of bedrooms and a sleeping loft or bunk room. The kitchen has a handy, tucked-in pantry with a wraparound counter for working space, a serving area and bar stools. The bathroom has a large vanity and linen storage. The entry has its own grand foyer for a more formal appearance.

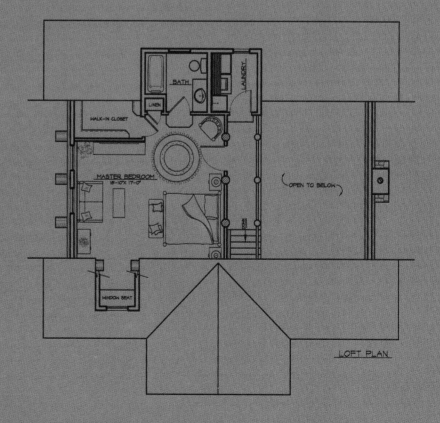

FRONT ELEVATION

LOFT PLAN

REAR ELEVATION

3 bedrooms

2 bathrooms

No basement

1,400 square feet

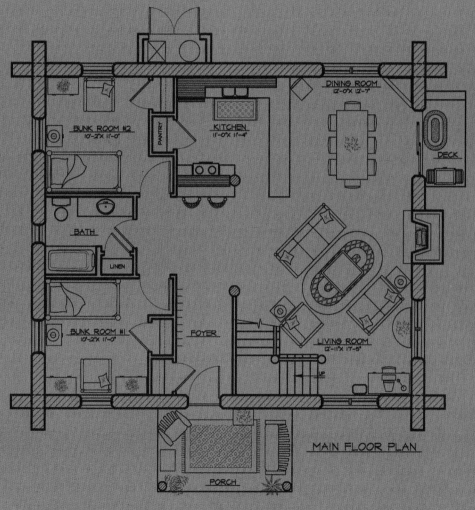

BUNK ROOM #2
10'-2"X 11'-0"

KITCHEN
11'-0"X 11'-4"

PANTRY

DINING ROOM
12'-0"X 12'-7"

DECK

BATH

LINEN

BUNK ROOM #1
10'-2"X 11'-0"

FOYER

LIVING ROOM
12'-11"X 17'-5"

MAIN FLOOR PLAN

PORCH

Whitney Point

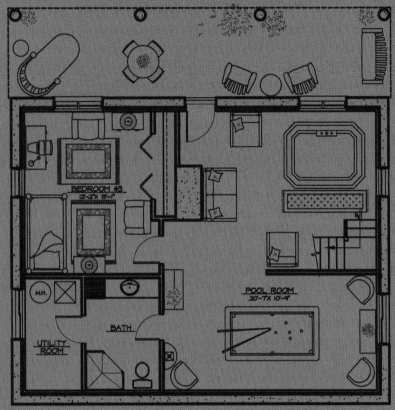

3 bedrooms

3 bathrooms

Full walk-out basement (additional 1,008 square feet)

1,500 square feet (above ground)

BEDROOM #3
12-2"X 5-4"

POOL ROOM
20-7"X 10-4"

W.H.

BATH

UTILITY
ROOM

BASEMENT PLAN

This plan explodes in size by making use of a walkout basement. This is another plan that one of our clients asked us to customize to fit their young family's needs. They wanted a camp design that would capture the southern views to their advantage for the north country's hard winters. There are three bathrooms, one on each floor, to accommodate the large family.

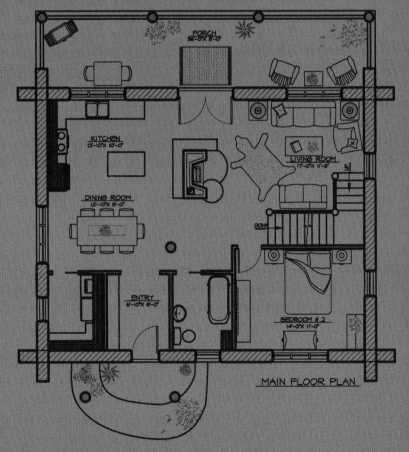

PORCH
16-0"X 6-0"

KITCHEN
12-10"X 10-0"

LIVING ROOM
17-0"X 11-8"

DINING ROOM
12-10"X 6-0"

DOWN

ENTRY
6-10"X 5-0"

BEDROOM #2
14-0"X 11-0"

MAIN FLOOR PLAN

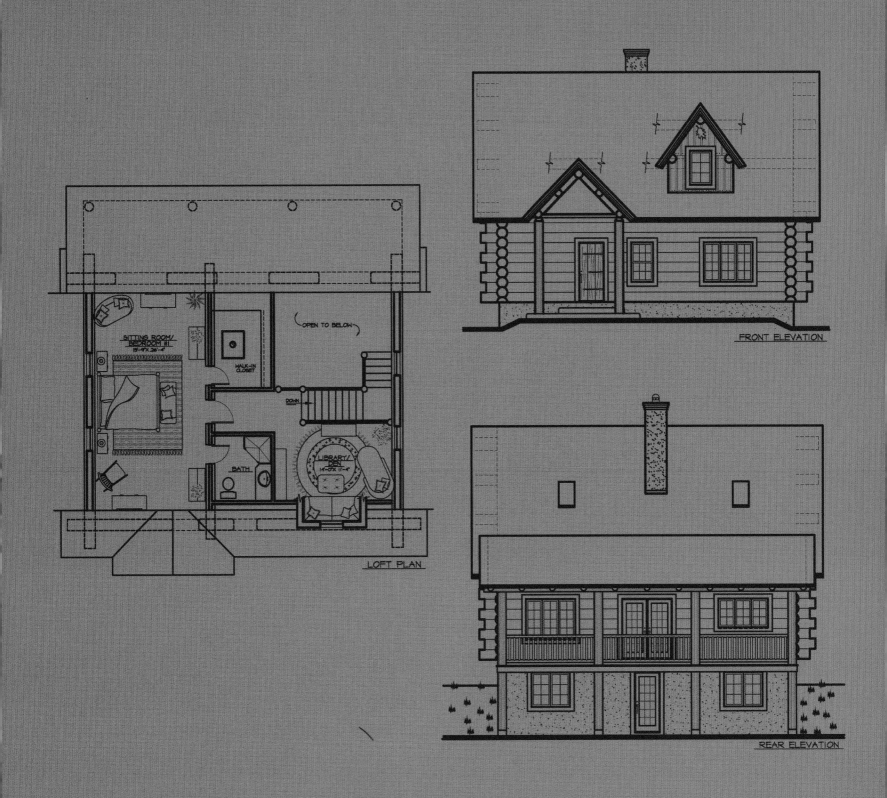

SITTING ROOM/
BEDROOM #1
13'-9 X 26'-4

WALK-IN
CLOSET

OPEN TO BELOW

DOWN

BATH

LIBRARY/
DEN
14'-0 X 17'-4

LOFT PLAN

FRONT ELEVATION

REAR ELEVATION

Mad River Camp

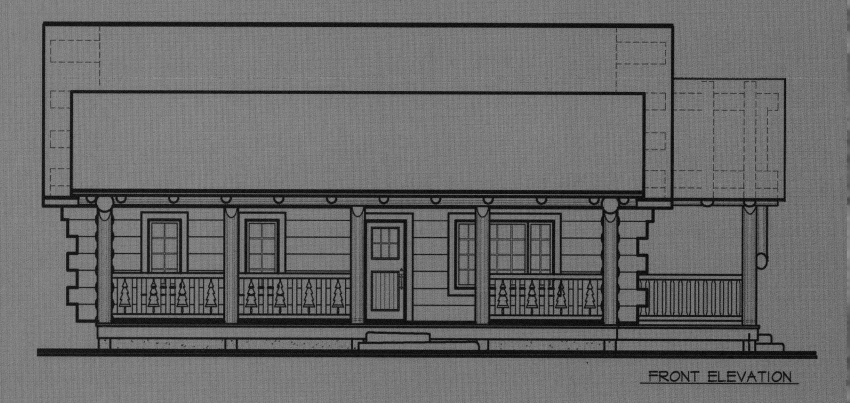

FRONT ELEVATION

This two-bedroom camp has a shared bathroom with linen storage and a stacked washer and dryer. The ceiling is flat but tall, soaring to 9 feet 6 inches on average. The ceiling is decorated with large-diameter ceiling joists that span over the living room and kitchen area for added interest, then the ceiling drops down over the bedroom and bath areas. Two porches add outdoor living for different times of the day.

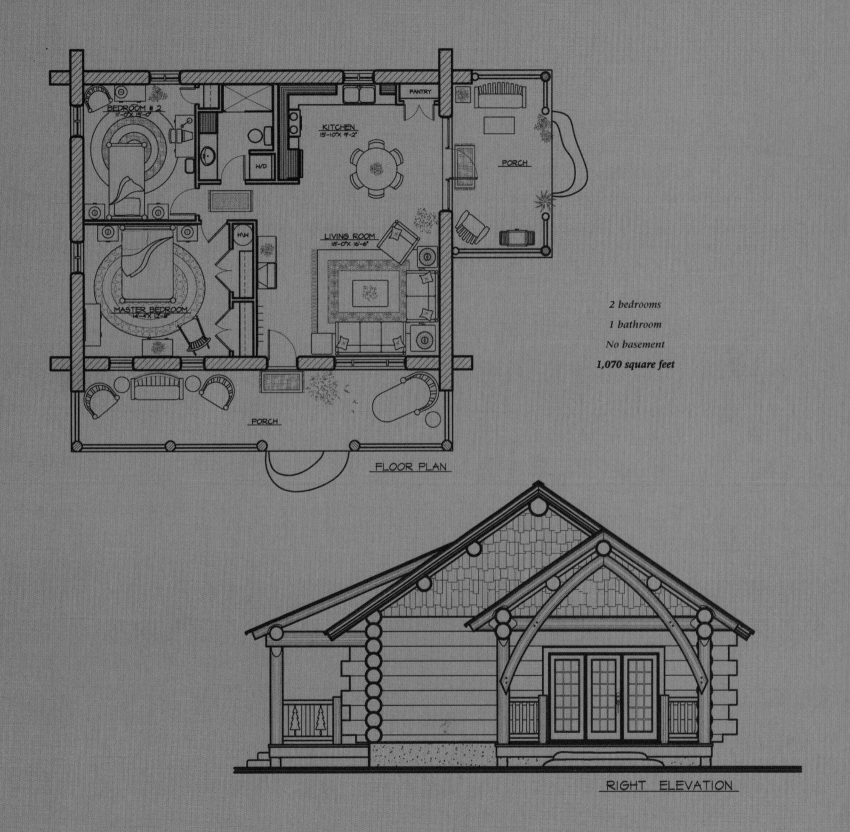

BEDROOM #2
11'-10" X 15'-0"

KITCHEN
15'-10" X 9'-2"

PANTRY

PORCH

W/D

HW

MASTER BEDROOM
14'-4" X 12'-8"

LIVING ROOM
18'-0" X 16'-6"

2 bedrooms

1 bathroom

No basement

1,070 square feet

PORCH

FLOOR PLAN

RIGHT ELEVATION

Camp Dragonfly

Typical of many homes in the Adirondacks is the graceful hip-roof design. This home was inspired by a very old camp in the Adirondacks that was sided with elm-bark shingles and wrapped in a four-sided porch, allowing outdoor living to be enjoyed any time of day. The camp has four camp-style bedrooms with intersecting dormers that carve out additional light and usable space into the sloping roofline. Although storybook detailing is in its design, the camp is very complicated to construct. With the added detail comes the additional cost of construction.

REAR ELEVATION

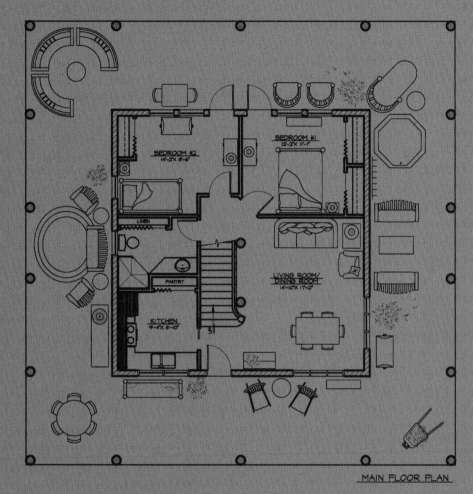

BEDROOM #2
14'-2"x 8'-6"

BEDROOM #1
12'-2"x 11'-1"

LINEN

PANTRY

LIVING ROOM/
DINING ROOM
14'-10"x 17'-2"

KITCHEN
9'-0"x 8'-10"

MAIN FLOOR PLAN

4 bedrooms

2 bathrooms

No basement

1,500 square feet

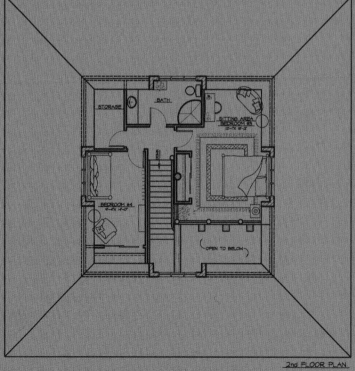

STORAGE

BATH

SITTING AREA
BEDROOM #3
12'-0"x 15'-2"

BEDROOM #4
14'-0"x 14'-0"

OPEN TO BELOW

2nd FLOOR PLAN

Au Sable Camp

This cabin has ceilings that soar up 23 feet to a sleeping loft or bunk room. Although this stock plan was based on another called Whistling Crow, a new client asked for the plan to be customized to fit his lifestyle and love of curtain design elements. The interior ceiling has exposed log rafters about 4 feet on center for an interesting rhythm of added architecture. The camp has several porches and open decks to create a mix of outdoor rooms. The exterior railings are designed in the famous Adirondack free-form style. Note that before building a free-form style of railing, you must check your local building code as this style of railing does not meet national code requirements.

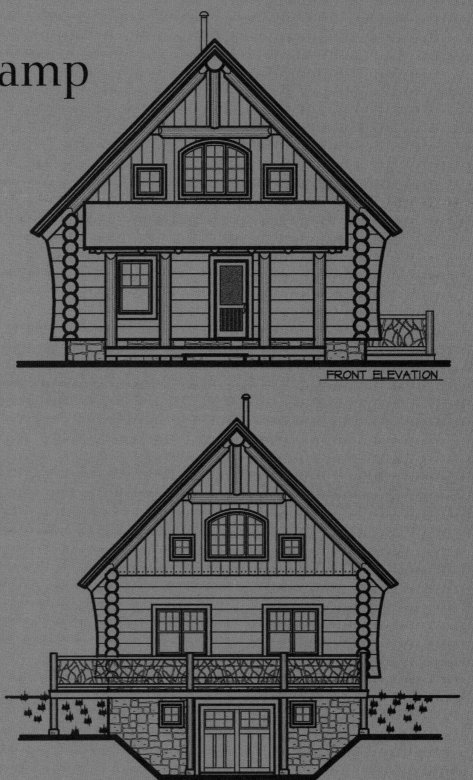

FRONT ELEVATION

BACK ELEVATION

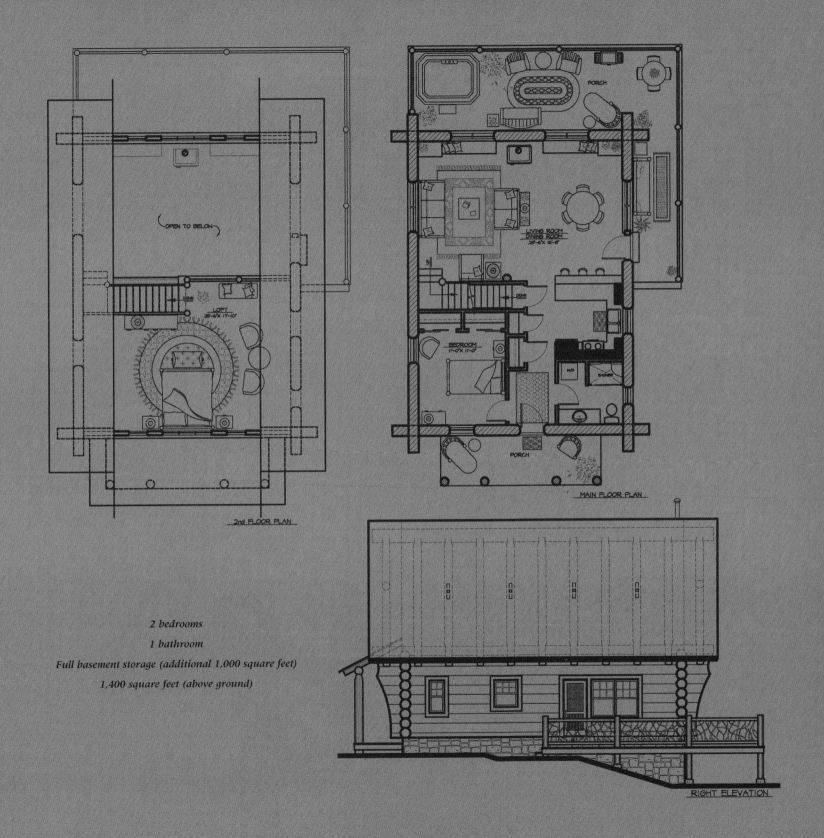

OPEN TO BELOW

LOFT
25'-6"X 17'-10"

2nd FLOOR PLAN

PORCH

LIVING ROOM
DINING ROOM
25'-6"X 16'-8"

BEDROOM
11'-0"X 11'-0"

PORCH

MAIN FLOOR PLAN

2 bedrooms

1 bathroom

Full basement storage (additional 1,000 square feet)

1,400 square feet (above ground)

RIGHT ELEVATION

Sugar Hill

The camp is small but sweet. This two-bedroom camp could sleep up to eight people with the use of a pull-out sofa or futon. The refrigerator tucks into the wall, allowing for the most countertop space. The staircase to the loft curls around the large fireplace. The basement adds plenty of additional storage and can also be customized to different uses that better accommodate lifestyles and needs.

RIGHT ELEVATION

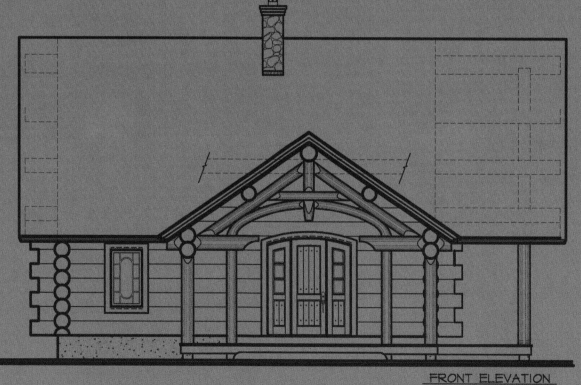

FRONT ELEVATION

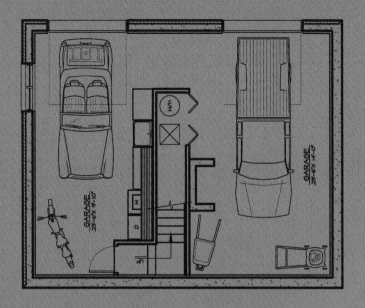

2 bedrooms

1 bathroom

Full basement storage (additional 832 square feet)

1,012 square feet (above ground)

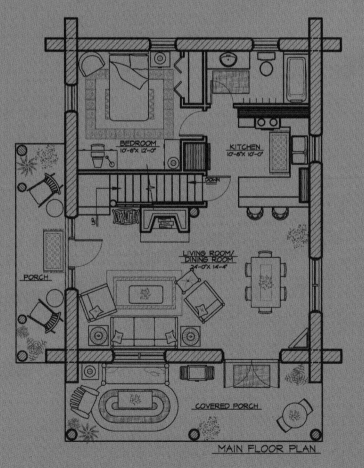

GARAGE
23'-6" X 9'-10"

GARAGE
23'-6" X 14'-0"

BEDROOM
10'-8" X 12'-0"

KITCHEN
10'-8" X 10'-0"

PORCH

LIVING ROOM/
DINING ROOM
24'-0" X 14'-4"

COVERED PORCH

MAIN FLOOR PLAN

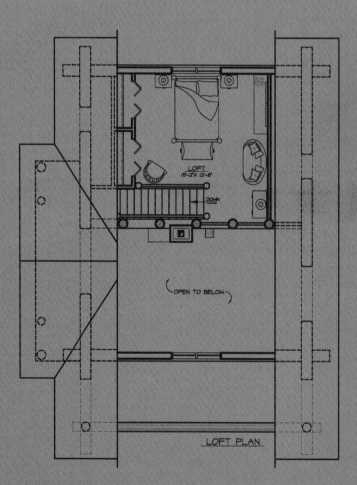

LOFT
15'-2" X 12'-8"

OPEN TO BELOW

LOFT PLAN

Echo Canyon

This is the same layout as Mad River Camp (on page 110–11), transformed into a log-element structure. The plan has been one of our most popular and most customized to date. Everyone looks at the plan and asks for their signature style to be added. The camp is also one of the most cost-effective layouts to construct. This plan is simple yet classic, with plenty of room for fun, family and friends.

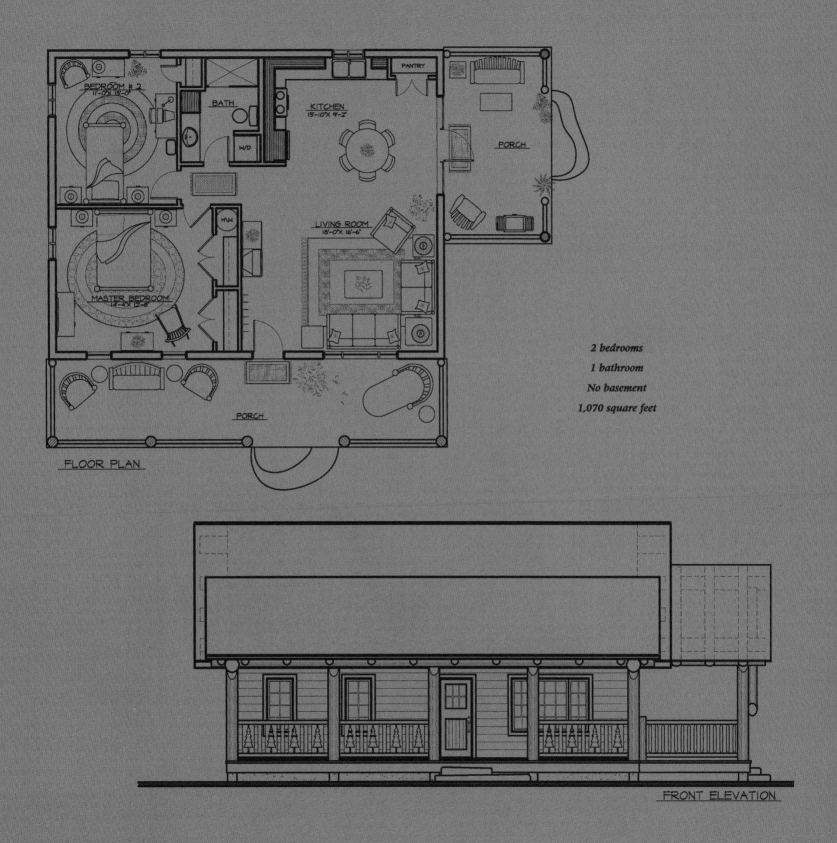

BEDROOM # 2
11'-0"X 13'-0"

BATH

KITCHEN
15'-10"X 9'-2"

PANTRY

PORCH

W/D

HW

LIVING ROOM
18'-0"X 16'-6"

MASTER BEDROOM
14'-4"X 12'-8"

PORCH

FLOOR PLAN

2 bedrooms

1 bathroom

No basement

1,070 square feet

FRONT ELEVATION

Wolf Point

This two-bedroom, two-bathroom camp is all contained within a single-floor camp design. Every inch is evaluated for flow and function; it has large bedroom closets and a stacked washer and dryer. The ceiling is flat overhead with large log ceiling joists as decorative elements. This style of roof allows for conventionally built roof rafters that help keep construction costs down as well as hide additional lighting and mechanicals.

2 bedrooms
1 bathroom
No basement
1,053 square feet

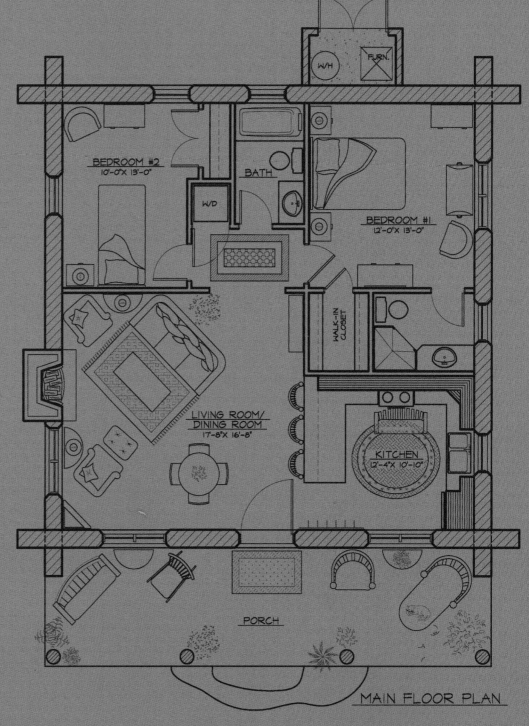

MAIN FLOOR PLAN

FRONT ELEVATION

BACK ELEVATION

Cedar Point

This is the same layout as Indian Lake on page 106–7, but converted into a log-element structure. This classic layout packs three bedrooms and two baths within a minimum footprint. The layout is efficient and has great flow and functionality. With just a change of window grille patterns and exterior siding materials, this home could drastically change in look, transforming into many styles.

FRONT ELEVATION

RIGHT ELEVATION

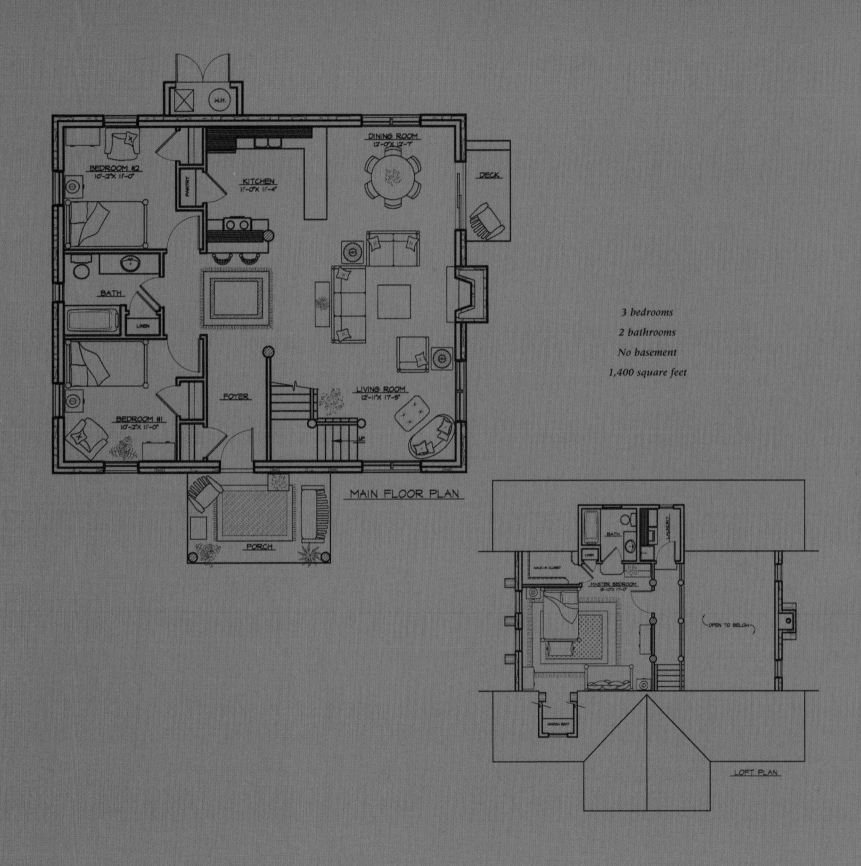

BEDROOM #2
10'-2" X 11'-0"

DINING ROOM
12'-0" X 12'-7"

DECK

KITCHEN
11'-0" X 11'-4"

PANTRY

BATH

LINEN

LIVING ROOM
12'-11" X 17'-5"

FOYER

UP

BEDROOM #1
10'-2" X 11'-0"

3 bedrooms

2 bathrooms

No basement

1,400 square feet

MAIN FLOOR PLAN

PORCH

BATH

LAUNDRY

WALK-IN CLOSET

LINEN

MASTER BEDROOM
15'-10" X 17'-0"

OPEN TO BELOW

WINDOW SEAT

LOFT PLAN

Eagle's Bay (continued)

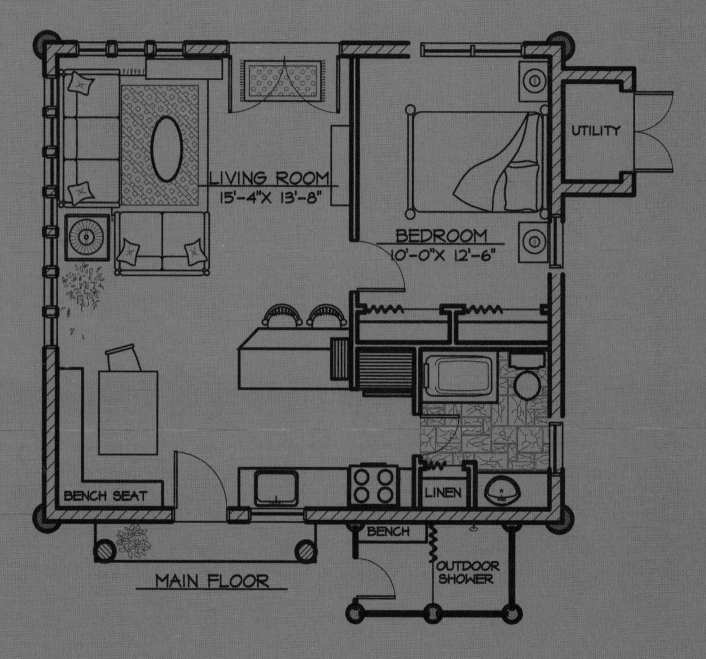

LIVING ROOM
15'-4"X 13'-8"

BEDROOM
10'-0"X 12'-6"

UTILITY

BENCH SEAT

LINEN

MAIN FLOOR

BENCH

OUTDOOR
SHOWER

Resources

Many log handcrafters and timber framers do not advertise in magazines, newspapers or the phone book. Most log builders and timber framers are artists who prefer to be outdoors and not tied to a desk. A very large majority of handcrafters have small operations, as it is difficult to deal with all the general business details that are generated by running a large company.

The International Log Builders' Association and The Timber-Framers Guild are educational associations for handcrafted log construction and timber framing organizations for builders and related trades. The associations have a long list of members from around the world. The International Log Builders' Association has conferences a few times a year for professional builders and related trades. Their conferences are held at different locations throughout the United States and Canada.

International Log Builders'
Association
P.O. Box 775
Lumby, BC, Canada V0E 2G0
www.logassociation.org
250.547.8776
800.532.2900

The Timber-Framers Guild
P.O. Box 60
Becket, MA 01223
www.tfguild.org
888.453.0879

BLUEPRINT PRICE INFORMATION:
Beaver Creek Design Services
35 Territory Road
Oneida, NY 13483
www.beavercreekloghomes.com
www.beavercreekdesignservices.com
315.245.4112

Log Home Storybook Collection
(1,000–1,999 square feet):
5 Sets...............$845.00
8 Sets...............$895.00

Log Home Estate Collection
(2,000–2,999 square feet):
5 Sets...............$945.00
8 Sets...............$995.00

All prices are subject to change without notice.

All plans are subject to shipping and handling cost.

Orders should be made carefully. All plans are specifically printed for each client, with no refunds available.

Photographer's Acknowledgments

A word of kind thanks to the owners of the inns, lodges, and fine Adirondack accommodations who graciously allowed my photos to be published in the book. They include:
- Lake Placid Lodge (www.lakeplacidlodge.com) pages 9, 21, 42–43, 45, 49, 64, 65, 67, 68, 69, 76–77, 82–83, 86–87, 102, 103, inside cover.
- The Mirror Lake Inn (www.mirrorlakeinn.com) pages 25, 53, 69.
- The Point (<http://www.thepointresort.com>) pages 24, 58.
- Morningside Camps and Cabins (www.morningsidecamps.com) pages 39, back cover.
- The Waldheim (www.waldheim.com) page 46.
- Garnet Hill Lodge (www.garnet-hill.com) page 66.
- The Hedges (www.thehedges.com) page 85.
- Adirondak Loj (www.adk.org) page 98.

Additionally, the photographs of White Pine Camp appearing on pages 23, 66, and 96 are used with permission of White Pine Camp Associates, LLP. For information on historic tours and cabin rentals at White Pine camp please visit www.whitepinecamp.com.

Among historic establishments and sites, The Adirondack Museum in Blue Mountain Lake (www.adirondackmuseum.org) permitted use of images on pages 2–3, 33, and 92.

Camp Santanoni (www.aarch.org) appears on page 51; and the Visitors Interpretive Center in Paul Smiths is on page 20.

Two fine stores, the Ray Brook Frog (www.raybrookfrog,com) page 10–11, and the Birch Store in Keene Valley (www.birchstore.com) are envisioned herein.

The various camp owners at Otis Mountain: the Jeffers, the Daniels, the Frisbies, and the Sigels; also property owners: the Bettes, the Grahams, the Rosenthals, the Liebers, the DeVoes, the Barlows, and the Bissells are due many thanks for letting me share glimpses of their cabins within the book.

Those who enabled access, provided information or simply showed faith in my vision include Adirondack Life magazine, the New York Times, Scheefer Builders, David Rogers Cabinetry, the Rolands, Elizabeth Folwell, Kathryn Kincannon, Adele Connors/Advertisers Workshop, Maggie Bartley, and noted author and partner in this project Robbin Obomsawin.

Naj, John, Rachel, Tony, David, the Catillazes, and the kids at Connery thanks for being there! Ed, pups = ☺

On the front cover: Lake Placid boathouse at Camp Chipmunk.
On the back cover: cabin and bridge at Morningside Camps and Cabins.
Inside front photo: cabin on Lake Placid, Lake Placid Lodge.